A CHILD PSYCHOTHERAPY PRIMER
Suggestions for the Beginning Therapist

A CHILD PSYCHOTHERAPY PRIMER
Suggestions for the Beginning Therapist

Josiah B. Dodds, Ph.D.

School of Professional Psychology
University of Denver
Denver, Colorado

HUMAN SCIENCES PRESS, INC.
72 FIFTH AVENUE
NEW YORK, N.Y. 10011

Printed in the United States of America
987654321

Library of Congress Cataloging in Publication Data

Dodds, Josiah B.
  A child psychotherapy primer.

  Bibliography: p.159
  Includes index.
  1. Child psychotherapy. I. Title. [DNLM: 1. Psycho-
therapy—in infancy & childhood. WS 350.2 D642c]
  RJ504.D57 1985   618.92′89′14   84-27860
  ISBN 0-89885-240-4 (hardcover)
      0-89885-310-9 (paperback)

CONTENTS

ACKNOWLEDGMENTS

First my thanks go to my students who ask difficult questions and who do not accept simple answers. Dr. Carla Garrity, Dr. Barbara Martinez, and Dr. Dorothy Todd made particularly helpful suggestions as they read through a draft of this work. I am grateful to Mrs. Addie Cohen for editing this manuscript. Most of all, though, the real credit for this effort goes to the children I have seen in the therapy room and who have become my friends. They have taught me much.

All names and other identifying information have been fictionalized throughout the text. Resemblance to any persons, living or dead, is not intended.

INTRODUCTION

The purpose of this book is to assist students to deal with the practical issues of child psychotherapy. The questions addressed here are those students frequently ask when they start seeing children in mental health settings. The questions and discussions are most applicable to therapy methods calling for a one-to-one relationship between a psychotherapist and a child, rather than to methods such as family and group therapy. Though the issues raised are largely the concerns of therapists who are beginning to learn various play therapy techniques, many questions are relevant to beginning therapists who are learning other intervention methods, such as behavior modification, cognitive therapy, and direct counseling. The issues are those encountered by any psychotherapist when relating to a child and to other people in the child's life.

The answers to the questions raised here offer some commonsense suggestions. They are not meant to be complete. Perhaps in some cases you will disagree with the suggestions, but my purpose will be fulfilled if they stimulate you to consider the issues involved and to arrive at your own reasoned positions.

Generally, I have attempted to be atheoretical except where a particular theoretical orientation is specifically stated. However, since it is both impossible and undesirable to operate with no theory, some of my basic beliefs are given here. Few people, psychologists included, are satisfied with the labels others place on them, yet most are loath to label themselves. I am no exception, but with the usual reservations I currently accept the adjectives humanistic-existential with a helping of psychodynamic and just a sprinkling of behavioristic. If you label yourself with different labels or with widely differing proportions of these labels, you will undoubtedly find yourself in disagreement with much of what follows.

One of the few books on child psychotherapy available at the time I started my training (early 1960s) was Frederick Allen's *Psychotherapy with Children* (1942). This man's wisdom and basic attitude toward children have greatly influenced me. Along with Allen, I believe that children, and adults for that matter, have within them fundamental tendencies for growth toward health. "Growth toward health" is defined here as becoming more flexible, moving toward more complex levels of psychological organization, growing more positive in feeling and learning more adaptable ways of meeting life's stresses. Often this growth tendency is blocked. I believe that given the proper opportunity a child will find his or her own growth-fostering ways to deal with stress. Such an opportunity is optimally attained in a therapy relationship in which the therapist both supports the child—that is, gives the child unconditional positive regard—and gives the child freedom to explore him/herself and interpersonal relationships. In my view the therapist cannot and should not attempt to maintain the role of a totally neutral, blank screen. The therapist represents reality to the child and sets limits on the child's overt behavior. The therapist becomes involved in a complex relationship with the child and reacts as a real person to the child. I believe that the therapist's human reactions are the fabric out of which the therapy is built.

The therapist also must think. I believe that I can be potentially more helpful to the child if I have a clear theoretical model and continually ask questions about why the child is behaving in certain ways, how the child came to these behaviors, what interventions would best help the child overcome his/her problems, and how I know the child is making any progress. I obtain clues to some of the answers to these questions by monitoring my emotional reactions as I interact with the child. I believe, then, that the therapist needs to operate simultaneously on three tracks: cognitive, emotional, and interactional.

Chapter 1

GENERAL CONSIDERATIONS

WHAT IS CHILD PSYCHOTHERAPY?

Child psychotherapy is the process whereby a child is helped in a relationship with a psychotherapist to resolve emotional, behavioral, or interpersonal problems. The process is designed to change the child in some way, either to ease internal pain, change undesirable behavior, or improve relationships between the child and other people who are important in the child's life. Change in the child is effected by a variety of methods. Commonly used methods are a range of behavior modification techniques, many forms of play therapy, family therapy of different models, directive counseling, and cognitive therapies. There are other less direct methods of helping a child change, such as parent counseling and manipulation of the child's environment, but they are not generally considered to be child psychotherapy. Issues involved in these methods will not be considered in this book. Certainly many other relationships and experiences the child has can be "therapeutic," that is, can ease intrapsychic pain, change behavior, and alter the nature of interpersonal relationships. So what differentiates psychotherapy? All methods of child psychotherapy require the establishment of a therapeutic relationship between the child and a mental health professional. This relationship differs from all others.

WHAT IS THE NATURE OF THE CHILD-THERAPIST RELATIONSHIP IN PSYCHOTHERAPY?

The relationship between the child and adult in psychotherapy is different from other relationships the child has. It is easier to discuss what the therapy relationship is not than what it is. It is unlike the child-parent, the child-playmate, the child-teacher, the child-big brother/sister, and the child-older-relative relationships. There are, however, some elements of each of these relationships in the child-therapist relationship. Not only can the child transfer portions of these relationships into the therapy relationship but the therapist also acts like these people in some ways. For example, to the degree that the therapist sets limits to insure the child's and therapist's safety, he/she is like a parent. To the degree that he/she interacts with the child in games and free play, the therapist is like a playmate. To the degree that the therapist conveys support and positive feelings to a child with whom the therapist has a special relationship, he/she is like an older relative.

Just as the child-therapist relationship is not devoid of elements that characterize other relationships of the child, these other relationships are not devoid of the elements characterizing the child-therapist relationship. What characterizes the child-therapist relationship grows out of the therapist's attitude and behavior with the child. The therapist accepts most of the child's behavior and all of the child's thoughts and feelings with a nonjudgmental, supportive attitude. The therapist places a high positive value on the child's right to these thoughts and feelings. The time in the interaction between therapist and child is spent focusing on the child's behavior, perceptions, fantasies, and feelings rather than on the therapist's, with the goal of helping the child to achieve more mature and adaptive ways of adjusting to life's stresses. Underlying the child-therapist relationship is a professional contract between a helper and a helpee that differentiates it from family relationships, which are maintained primarily on love and/or obligation, and that differentiates it from relationships with playmates, which are based on the mutual exchange of friendship. A professional contract also underlies the teacher-child relationship, but the teacher is generally expected to impart knowledge and skills in the cognitive realm directly to the child and to be less focused on the child's feelings and fantasies.

WHAT IS THE DIFFERENCE BETWEEN CHILD PSYCHOTHERAPY AND PLAY THERAPY?

Play therapy is one method of psychotherapy that may be used in helping a child resolve problems. Play therapy is more of a technique than a cohesive theory. Some workers in the field believe that any free play with an adult will be beneficial for the child; that is, they believe that given an unstructured environment with an accepting adult the child will inevitably work out his/her problems. The accepting adult, a play therapist, would not necessarily need to be a trained child psychotherapist.

Others in the field, including myself, do not have as much faith in the hypothesis that unrestricted play alone is always sufficient for resolving the child's problems; they plan ways to intervene in helping to solve the problems. Play may be one of the methods used. It would be instituted with a rationale that would fit the clinician's conceptualization of the child's problem and the means of intervention.

The psychotherapist's conceptualization of the child's problem greatly influences the course of therapy even if it is "nondirective." The influence is through the responses the psychotherapist makes to the child's play, fantasy, and talk. The responses grow out of the psychotherapist's conception of the child's problems and what he/she thinks will help resolve the problems. Even the nondirective psychotherapist will convey these conceptualizations by selective attention to the child's behavior.

How Do Child Psychotherapy Theories Differ?

Child psychotherapy theories can differ greatly from one therapist to the next on several dimensions. The beginning student of child psychotherapy might find the following dimensions useful when comparing the various theories and techniques of child psychotherapy.

1. The child may be viewed as motivated from within (self-actualizer) or from without (reacting organism) or some balance of these two.
2. Particular therapeutic schools might call for special rooms, equipment, and materials.
3. The therapist may be more or less active in directing the child-therapist interaction.
4. The therapist may actively teach the child new skills, behaviors, and attitudes or let the child discover during the course of therapy new ways of behaving and new self-understandings.

5. The therapist may use his/her own feelings and emotional reactions during the session or attempt to remain emotionally neutral.
6. The therapist might encourage, discourage, or ignore transference phenomena in the child.

Whatever position along these dimensions any one child psychotherapist takes, they would all agree that the child's play is a means of communicating and that the therapy room equipment and materials are to facilitate that play communication.

WHAT IS A PLAY SESSION?

In layman's usage, a play session means any time period in which any play is occurring. It could be by one or more persons, by children or adults, with any materials and for any length of time. The use of the term in the mental health professions, however, has a more specific meaning. Usually the following conditions are present when the term play session is used in mental health circles:

1. At least one child, who is in the client role, and one adult, who is trained in some mental health profession, are present.
2. A place is designated as the place of play, usually a playroom or a designated part of a room such as an office.
3. A specified period of time, generally between 30 and 90 min., is set aside for the play.
4. Materials are present that encourage expressive behavior and imaginative activity of the child.

5. The focus of the adult's attention is primarily on the child's activities, thoughts and feelings.
6. A therapeutic relationship between the adult and the child is established.

WHEN IS THE PLAY METHOD APPROPRIATE?

The play method is most helpful for children with internal problems such as fears, anxieties, guilt, poor self-image, feeling of being deserted, jealousy, grief, and anger. The method is appropriate whenever the child's communication with the therapist can be facilitated through the medium of play. Anyone who has worked with children, especially young children, knows how difficult it can be for a child to talk about feelings and about the kinds of complex human interaction problems that often bring the child to the clinic. The young child's language and cognitive constructs are not sufficiently developed to express these concepts verbally. Developmentally, the child first expresses feelings and desires most easily through action, then later through fantasy, and finally through language (Santostefano 1971). If the clinician and child are in a setting that has play materials, the child can find a balance of expression through action, fantasy, and language. The reflective child will shift the modality of expression, or combination or modalities, from moment to moment. The playroom facilitates this motility of expressive means.

The older child's language and cognitive concepts may be sufficient for expression of feelings and interpersonal events, but the child may be too unpracticed or too uncomfortable to discuss these matters. For example, children often are not at ease sitting and talking face-to-face with an adult, especially a strange adult in an unfamiliar setting. In such cases focus on play materials and activities can place a comfortable barrier between the child and adult, thus helping the child avoid eye-to-eye, have-to-talk interaction until the child is ready.

AT WHAT AGES ARE PLAY TECHINIQUES APPROPRIATE?

Play techniques are generally used with children between 3 and 12 years of age, but there are exceptions either way at both ends of this range. Some 2-year-olds might profit from play therapy, just as some adults might. Then again, play may not be the most appropriate means of interacting with some 11-year-old children. As discussed above, play techniques are appropriate at any age at which they will facilitate or help regulate communication. One 9-year-old boy, coming into the playroom for the first time, remarked, "Are those dolls? Do I have to play with *dolls?*" "Not if you don't want to," I replied. After an interval so short it should have been embarrassing to him, the boy was busily engaged in doll play. Another boy, aged 12 and highly verbal, with whom I had worked for a year in the playroom, stopped one day at the door of an adult interview room and announced that he was ready to use the grown-up room to talk. He did and never retuned to the playroom.

Youngsters in the 12- and 13-year age group present a dilemma. They may feel insulted by being taken into a playroom, but they may feel extremely uncomfortable sitting in an adult interview room face-to-face with a strange adult. Here is a way that I have found useful to handle this dilemma. At the first session you might show the youngster the playroom *and* an adult consultation room and ask him/her which room he/she would feel most comfortable using. In order to remove social pressure you might say, while showing the child the rooms, "Some kids prefer to use this room and some prefer the other room.

It doesn't matter to me—we can use whichever you prefer. Also, we can change later if you wish." In any case, I will always have available in the adult consulting room and within reach of both of us some clay, a deck of cards, paper and colored felt-tip pens, and perhaps a game of checkers. You and the child might pick up some clay or the cards to fiddle with while you talk. What this does is leave the option open for the child to do what he/she is most comfortable doing.

In general, given the opportunity, children will answer the question of appropriateness of using play materials themselves. If they are in a room with some materials, they will use them or not as they feel comfortable. The answer to the question of when and at what age the play technique is appropriate is thus: If the child and the clinician can and wish to use play material to facilitate and ease their communication, then it is appropriate.

When Is the Play Method Not Appropriate?

Many children are brought to the mental health professional with problems that might be more effectively helped through techniques other than play. If the parent is unhappy with a child's behavior, such as not picking up his/her room, talking back, staying out past the time set for being home, and the like, then it is unreasonable to expect that play would necessarily change the child's behavior. Parent counseling or parent-child sessions would be a more direct means of tackling these kinds of problems. Similarly, if the primary complaint is a dysfunctional relationship with others, such as siblings, peers, or teachers, then intervention that involves both sides of the dyad is indicated.

You, as a child therapist, will be getting into a trap if you take on a child in play therapy acting as the agent of someone else, parent or teacher, who wants you to change the child's behavior. Perhaps as the child profits from play therapy by feeling better emotionally, by developing more mature and adaptive ways of dealing with internal and external stress, and by developing more positive self attitudes, the child's behavior with others will change for the better, but you cannot offer the parent or teacher a guarantee. To accept the child for therapy under these circumstances implies that you are accepting their goal for behavior change and therein lies the trap. The primary reason for using the play technique with a child is to help the child deal with internal problems, not to get him/her to change behavior that disturbs others.

Often children are brought to a mental health professional with a primary symptom such as bed-wetting, learning disability, or attention deficit and also with associated feelings of incompetence, shame, depression, and negative self-image. In these cases the approach could be twofold: (a) direct intervention on the symptom (e.g., bell and pad for bed wetting, remedial teaching for the learning disorder, or medication for the attention deficit) and (b) psychotherapy with play techniques to help the child change his/her concomitant negative feelings and attitudes.

Chapter 2

THERAPY ROOM AND MATERIALS

WHAT KIND OF ROOM IS BEST FOR THE USE OF PLAY TECHNIQUES?

Just about any space can be used for a therapy session. I have successfully conducted sessions in many different and difficult settings such as a 9-foot-by-9-foot office full of furniture plus two sit-in observers and a very active 6-year-old boy, in a small room in a trailer, and in a parochial school chapel (observed by Christ from the cross!). Since limits must be placed on the child by the therapist, particularly if the child needs help in learning to control his/her own impulses, the more childproof the room is the easier it is for both the therapist and the child. If the therapist uses an office with work papers on the desk, a blinking multiple-line telephone, potted plants on the windowsill, and fragile ornaments on the wall, an enormous amount of energy could be spent on limiting the child's behavior so as to protect those things. Few rooms are completely breakproof, but the therapist and child will both have a much easier time if the room is sturdy and does not contain easily damaged items.

If one were in a position to plan a therapy room in a new facility, the following features would make an ideal room. The room would be at least 8 feet by 12 feet to allow for some vigorous movement. The lights and windows would be unbreakable. If an observation glass is used, the microphone would be out of reach of the child and preferably not protruding into the room. Furniture would include a sturdy child-size table and two chairs plus a storage cabinet or shelves for standard toys and materials. A carpet on the floor adds comfort, but there should be bare tile floor at one end of the room for paint and water play. A sink with running water certainly adds convenience but is usually a luxury. If the walls are made of soft composition board, they will resist blows and knocks as well as being easily replaceable. It is helpful to have some storage space outside of the playroom for storing unused materials (so they do not clutter up the therapy room) and to safely keep projects or special materials for particular children.

What Materials Are Useful for Play Techniques?

Consider these two principles in selecting therapy materials:

1. The materials allow for as much flexibility in their use as possible so that the child may have the optimum conditions for self-expression. Contrast a Slinky with a piece of clay: The former has a limited number of possibilities—bouncing as a yo-yo, going down stairs and becoming bent and useless—whereas the clay (oil-base clay that does not dry out) has a long life and an infinite number of possibilities. The clay does not so much have meaning in itself as it attracts meaning projected onto it. Toys that

have movable (and therefore breakable) parts often draw the child into spending excessive therapy time manipulating a piece of machinery.

2. The materials offer the least possibility of harming the child, therapist, or room. If the limits set on the child's activity are those of not hurting the child, the therapist, or the room, then the more difficult it is to do this damage, the less likely the therapist and child will be spending time engaging in a struggle around limits. So one would avoid equipment such as darts with points (Velcro heads present few problems), punching bags that will swing up into the lights, hard balls that will break windows and heads, and guns that shoot missiles of some sort.

Each child therapist has a favorite set of play equipment; however, the beginner might consider the following:

1. Plastic materials: clay, sand, water, and fingerpaint. Play with water and fingerpaint is not recommended if the room is not equipped to cope easily with spillage.
2. Drawing materials: newsprint, crayons and pencils, possibly felt-tip pens, blackboard and chalk, tempera paints (again if adequate clean-up facilities are present).
3. Dolls in a simple dollhouse with simple, non-moving-part furniture. The standard doll family (mother, father, brother, sister, and baby) is used by some therapists, whereas others prefer to tailor the doll family constellation to reflect that in the child's household.
4. Hand puppets of people and/or animals.
5. Ball(s). (Child therapists the world over hail the invention of Nerf!)
6. Building blocks. If wood blocks are a problem, Styrofoam blocks are now available.

These additional items are found by many therapists to encourage self-expression and to facilitate communication: games, from simple games of chance to cards and chess; a set of play telephones; punching bag; gun; dress-up clothes; toy soldiers; play dishes; cars and trucks.

CAN SPECIFIC MATERIALS BE USED TO "LURE" THE CHILD INTO CERTAIN KINDS OF PLAY?

Yes, unless the therapist is operating from a *strictly* nondirective position. The degree of structure in introducing special materials for a given child may range from close to zero to a highly structured setup. An example of nonstructured use of special material would be placing a baby bottle and a baby doll on the playroom toy shelf for the child in whom one detects strong regressive and dependency pulls. The therapist's desire is to provide the material for projecting and acting out these themes. An example of a more structured use of special material would be providing a doll family constellation exactly matching the child's own family, then having the therapist act out the beginning of a scene that is salient for the child, such as a grandmother's death, and asking the child to continue playing out the scene.

The therapist often keeps in an out-of-the-way drawer or closet those materials to be pulled out for use with a particular child. I find plastic models particularly useful to facilitate interest and to promote give-and-take interaction between child and therapist. These are the rules I introduce to the child before starting work on the model:

1. "We must work on the model together."
2. "We leave the model here at the clinic until it is completed."
3. "You may take the model home to keep when it is assembled."

Should the Child Be Allowed to Bring Toys and Other Items from Home into the Therapy Room?

Why not?

Does Using Different Materials at Different Sessions or Changing Rooms Cause Problems?

I am repeatedly being surprised by children's sensitivity to changes within the therapy room or between rooms. Some children, of course, do not seem to give it a second thought, but many children appear to be uncomfortable with changes. Frequently, the children seen in therapy have experienced many negative or unreliable behaviors from others. As a result of these experiences, their level of trust in the consistency of people is low. For these children, changes in the therapy room could be interpreted as evidence that the clinic is unstable, including the relationship with the therapist. I am unaware of any empirical data on this point, but it seems like a reasonable clinical hypothesis.

The child does not have the cognitive structures that an adult uses to obtain consistency. Adults know they are in the same country, state, and section of town and they know (generally) what changes will be coming up in their living quarters or jobs. The adult has the geographical and time concepts for interpreting these things that the child under 11 probably does not. So the child may react with major feelings to changes that would be minor to the adult.

The practical implications of the child's sensitivity to change are that the therapist should try very hard to keep the same therapy room and the same play equipment in that room. Consistency in these things can contribute to the child's sense of continuity and security in the relationship with the therapist. With many other therapists using the same playroom and materials, it is not always easy to keep consistency. It might be wise for the therapist to check out the room before the child arrives for the session.

The therapist should not overlook the possibility of using deliberately planned change as a therapeutic tool. Changes could be used to reach goals such as increasing the child's tolerance for inconsistency, moving the child to a different kind of relationship with the therapist, and adding special equipment for getting at special problems in a child.

CAN THERAPY BE CONDUCTED OUTDOORS?

If therapeutic interactions are occurring between therapist and child, it makes little difference where they occur. However, if you wish to go outside the therapy room to conduct therapy, you might think about your reason for doing so. Is it to avoid observation by the supervisor? Is it to accomodate the child who wishes to flee the therapy room (and therapy)? Is it to play more vigorous games than is possible in the playroom? Is it to get treats to eat? Is it to enjoy the companionship of a walk together? In addition to understanding the reason(s) therapy moves outside, the beginning therapist might be aware of a few potential hazards.

1. Activities like catch, hide and seek, and Frisbee remove the therapist and child from easy verbal communication. Standing 20 feet apart and chasing balls makes it very difficult to explore verbally a child's feelings, fantasies, wishes, and attitudes, or to work out solutions to interpersonal problems. This may be exactly why the child wants to go outside and play ball.

2. Personal safety on city streets and parks is a concern. You should be particularly careful about exploring

the risks involved in transporting the child in your own vehicle. Perhaps your clinic does not have insurance to cover a possible liability suit from an accident occurring under such circumstances. You may decide that the reasons for going out outweigh the risks, but at least you need to weigh them consciously.

3. Obtaining snacks at neighborhood stores is an easy thing to do. Is it therapeutic? If you wish to, can you say no to the child after snacks are bought the first time?

Going outside the therapy room is tempting and easy to do. The most important thing is to be very clear about how it facilitates progress toward the goals of therapy for each particular child.

Chapter 3

INITIAL EVALUATION

How Is a Child Evaluated in a Play Session?

How one evaluates a child in a play session—that is, what information is sought, what behavior is noted, and particularly, how these are organized and interpreted—will depend to a large extent on one's theoretical orientation. The ego psychologist and the behaviorist will attend to different data or use the same data in different ways. However, the attempt here is to pull together some of those aspects of the child about which one may learn in a play session within a broad developmental theoretical framework. Later in this section the different uses of play session data within the psychoanalytic, phenomonological, behavioral, and cognitive models are noted.

Like the psychological test, the play interview is simply a way to obtain a sample of the child's behavior. The tasks presented to the child in a play interview are, of course, less structured than in tests. Nevertheless, the play session is far from unstructured and far from the child's natural life settings. Some child clinicians (e.g., Swanson 1970) feel that the evaluator should be more directive than the play therapist. The arguments are that the evaluator wants specific information (about family, school, friends, pets, etc.) and productions (drawings, wishes, ambitions, etc.) that, given a totally nondirective session, the child is not likely to produce. Not only is the information useful to understanding the child but so is the child's reaction to the request: refusal, hesitancy, anxiety, ready compliance, eagerness to please, and so on.

To evaluate a child, to know the meaning of the child's appearance and behavior, the clinician must have developmental norms in his/her head. The beginning clinician using standarized tests has the obvious advantage over the clinician gathering data in a play session in that the norms for the tester are all printed out in the tables. However, the well-standardized tests do not cover vast areas of personality, social, cognitive, and physical development, nor do they help in the kinds of judgments the skilled child clinician makes about synchronization and dyssynchronization of various aspects or lines of development and functioning within the child. Much guidance for the interpretation of the developmental meaning and appropriateness of the child's behavior in a play session may be found in the child development literature covering major developmental milestones (physical and motor development, cognitive stages, language, friendship patterns, parental relationships, etc.). However, the child clinician must acquire a far more refined sense of what is appropriate for children of different ages and how the different areas of the child's functioning work together. Generally, this knowledge is acquired through many many hours of contact with children.

Here are some things a clinician might learn about a child in a play session:

1. The child's physical appearance will of course be

noted immediately. The child's size and shape, how dressed and groomed, racial features, posture, and visible handicaps are all important in terms of the child's self-view and in terms of how others react to the child. Sometimes the child's appearance will suggest some physical problem, chronic or temporary. A few possibilities might be a jaundiced appearance, bruises, red eyes, or very lethargic behavior. If the clinician receives any suggestion of a physical problem, then collaboration with a physician is essential. Mental health professionals cannot afford to ignore the whole child; the physical condition has profound influence on the psychological condition.

2. The child's response when invited to leave the waiting room and to separate from the mother (or other familiar adult who brought the child) to come with a strange adult into a strange room will provide a wealth of information about the mother-child relationship, the child's way of responding to strange adults, the child's fear-adventure balance, individuation, and self-confidence.

3. Gross motor development will be noted as the child moves to the playroom. As the child manipulates the various play materials, note can be made of his/her fine motor skills. Of greater importance, perhaps, than the level of motor skill (unless it is far below expected age level) is the child's energy level. In a play session one notes how vigorously or lethargically the child moves about in the room and manipulates toys. *Caution:* Activity level in the playroom has many possible interpretations. If the child is at the high end of the energy scale, it may be because of anxiety about being in a strange room with a strange adult (state) or it may be a reflection of the child's usual level of activity in many settings (trait). Similarly, if the child operates at a low activity level, it may be the child's reaction to a new setting. For example, the child's style of coping with new situations might be characterized by a cautious approach or the child might be fearful of the examiner.

An example of low activity level that may arise more from internal than situational factors would be a child who cannot give him/herself permission to intrude into the environment (see Erik Erikson's 1959 description of modality for stage III, intrusion). The careful clinician will collect information on activity level over several sessions and check with the mother or others who know the child as to the child's activity level in a variety of other settings.

4. Habits and mannerisms that might interfere with the child's social or personal functioning should be noted, e.g., tics, behaviors that are socially disapproved, style of eye contact, etc.

5. How the child copes with a strange room, with a strange adult, and with unstructured instructions such as "You may play with whatever you wish" will reveal a great deal about the child. (For an extensive discussion of coping styles you are referred to Lois Murphy 1962; pp. 6, 7, 74, and chap. 15).

6. It is important to note the child's mood during the session as well as shifts in mood: fear, sadness, exuberance, boredom, excitement, and the like. The degree to which the child appears to be suffering from the presenting problem also should be judged.

7. If the child is nonverbal during the play session, the clinician should note the following: (a) what the child chooses to play with; (b) the content of the play (themes); (c) the mode of the play (see Erik Erikson 1959 for modes and modalities such as suspicious, retentive, intrusive, making); (d) the child's impulse-control capacities; (e) the child's ability to concentrate and hold attention; (f) the emotions the child expresses, either directly or through the play; and (g) the child's actual competence and perceived self-competence in dealing with the playroom situation and materials.

8. If the child is verbal during the play session, the clinician, in addition to noting the above, can often obtain

much of the following: (a) the child's fears, (b) the child's wishes and dreams, and (c) the child's perception of his/her relationships with and his/her attitudes toward parents, siblings, peers, teachers, and self.

9. The child's relationship with the clinician may be revealing of how the child relates with other adults: how dependent, how fearful, how trusting, how much involvement with the clinician, how much the child seeks to please the clinician, how much the child seeks approval from the clinician. *Caution*: If the child is of a different racial, ethnic, or social class background from that of the clinician, then the meaning of the child's behaviors with the clinician and with the play materials must be interpreted in light of the child's reactions to these differences and of his/her own cultural norms. When the clinician is unfamiliar with the expected behavior of children in a particular group and typical reactions to outgroup members, it is incumbent on the clinician to obtain consultation from professionals who are familiar with the racial, ethnic, or social group to which the child belongs. If the clinician judges the child according to the clinician's own group norms, some gross misjudgments might be made in such areas as trust, deference, intrusiveness, exploratory behavior, and language development.

10. The manner of the child's behavior toward the clinician and with the play materials can often give clues as to the degree of egocentrism versus allocentrism in the child's perception of self and the world.

11. A notion may be gained by observing the child at play, particularly if the child is verbal, as to the child's level of cognitive development. Clues come from how the child organizes the materials, how symbolic the child's productions are, and how elaborate the child's fantasy associations are. *Caution:* Do not fall into the trap into which many child workers fall, namely, the belief that verbal fluency is positively correlated with intelligence. Observing the child play

with standard play items in a standard playroom is not a very reliable or valid way to obtain a notion of a child's level of cognitive development. Special materials are needed to test such Piagetian concepts as conservation, object permanence, classification, and level of representation; to test cognitive styles such as focal attention, field articulation, levelings, sharpening, and equivalence range; and to test "general intelligence."

From the point of view of a developmental model, the information about a child obtained in a play interview can be extremely useful in constructing a profile of the child's functioning across many areas of development. In addition to the child's appearance, the content of the child's problems, and the perceptions the child has of self and important interpersonal relationships, the clinician can obtain an indication of the child's age level in the following developmental lines: attachment and individuation from mother, coping with new environment, coping with strange adult, language usage, modality of expression (action, fantasy, language), play content, play organization, attention span, fears appropriate to age, perception of time, and emotional independence.

In assessing a child brought for professional help the clinician will, of course, not rely exclusively on the play interview material to make intervention recommendations. The child may function quite differently in different settings, and the clinician should attempt to ascertain how the child adapts in other environments. The play interview, for example, does not yield very good information about a child's social skills with peers, about his/her behavior within the family, or about the details of his/her cognitive development. Also, the play content in an initial session is often devoid of significant emotional content or perceptions of phenomena in the child's life outside the playroom. To assess these areas the clinician would consider other data-gathering techniques such as parent interview, teacher interview, family session, home observation, school observation including free play with peers, and special cognitive tests and projective tests.

If, on construction of a developmental profile, the child shows some lines of development far deviant from others, the clinician might wish to use the GAP diagnostic label "Developmental Deviations, deviations in maturational patterns" or one of the Axis II Developmental Disorders in DSM III. From the developmental point of view, however, constructing a profile will enable the clinician to move far beyond a diagnostic label and into recommending some intervention strategies based on the child's strengths and weaknesses and knowledge of the settings in which these strengths and weaknesses are exhibited.

Although the play interview method lends itself well to a developmental model, it does not lend itself equally well to use within all psychological models. Child evaluators with a psychoanalytic ego-psychology orientation and a phenomenological orientation will find the technique more useful than will the cognitively or behaviorally oriented evaluator. Below is a brief indication of how an evaluative play interview might be used by theorists of the four major schools.

Psychoanalytic Ego Psychology Theory

The ego-psychoanalytic theorists would take special note of material from which could be inferred the child's level of psychosexual development, predominant modality, sexual and aggressive drive level, guilt, object relations and range, and strength and modulation of defenses. For an elaboration of how a child's play productions can be used to assess these constructs, see Menninger Foundation, Children's Division (1969, pp. 176–213) and Freud (1977).

Phenomenological (Humanistic-Existential) Theory

The phenomenological theorist would make a special effort to understand the child's phenomenological interpretation of his/her world. This theorist would attempt to understand the child's level of self-awareness and experiences and the degree of his/her sensitivity to these experiences. The existential-humanist would look to find any factors that might block the child's effective functioning and growth in interpersonal relationships and in manipulating the environment. Of particular interest to the phenomenological theorist would be the child's concept of self. Actually, a formal evaluation such as obtained in the kind of evaluative play session that has been discussed here within the developmental framework is not that important for the existential-humanistic child therapist. That is, without evaluation the therapist of this persuasion would immediately set out to create the accepting atmosphere within the playroom wherein the child could learn to accept him/herself and unfold his/her growth potential (see Moustakas 1953, 1959, and Axline 1947).

Behavior Theory

The behavior theorist is less likely to use the play interview as an evaluation technique than is the developmental, phenomenological, or psychoanalytic theorist. The preferred technique would be to inquire about or observe the child in real-life situations in order to discover the environmental stimuli and reinforcers of the target behavior. If the child were seen in a play session, the behavior theorist would focus on the events surrounding and triggering the primary symptom (e.g., aggressive behavior, spacing-out episodes, habits, overdependency) and possibly also discover what reinforces the behavior. A description of the child or a developmental profile evolved from a play interview would not be focused enough to be very useful to the behaviorist.

Cognitive Theory

The cognitive theorist would probably need special equipment in order to ascertain the child's cognitive constructs, particularly if the child were nonverbal. If the child talks, the examiner would ask specific questions designed to learn the child's constructs and developmental level of cognitive functioning. If the child were nonverbal, special equipment would be needed to determine the constructs a child is capable of using. For example, one cannot judge a nonverbal child's capacity to classify if the child does not have classifiable objects in the playroom to manipulate. The cognitive theorist would tend then to move from an unstructured play interview to a structured, task-oriented interview much like a psychological test (see Santostefano 1971).

WHY MAKE EVALUATION AND THERAPY SEPARATE PROCESSES?

The answer to this question depends on the model and the operation of the clinic or child clinician. Certainly if the clinic's or clinician's practice is to make a formal psychodiagnostic classification of the child's disorder, then a time is set where all available information is examined and a diagnosis determined. The diagnostic and treatment processes are generally viewed as discrete operations.

On the other hand, a case may be made that treatment begins from the first contact the family has with the clinic or clinician and that evaluation goes on continually throughout treatment. The clinician certainly has an impact on the child during the initial contacts, and the process may prove helpful to the client. Other clinicians must have shared my astonishment when, after one or two sessions, a client offers thanks for curing the problem when the intent has been simply to evaluate the problem. During treatment the therapist should be continually formulating hypotheses and checking them out against the continually accumulating data from the therapy sessions, a kind of continuous diagnostic process.

Even if one views evaluation and treatment as one continuous process, it is useful to set some point in time at which those involved with the referral problem sit down with all of the accumulated information, formulate for themselves the reasons for the difficulty and plan what interventions may be helpful. This session may be with or without the family but certainly must include the family in implementing any treatment plans. If this discrete step is not taken, the child clinician might drift into work with the child with no clear understanding—and certainly no clear understanding on the family's and child's part—about just what the purpose of the play sessions is. Without such a purpose it is difficult to know what progress has been made and when treatment should be terminated.

WHAT ARE THE ADVANTAGES AND DISADVANTAGES OF THE SAME PERSON DOING THE INITIAL EVALUATION AND SUBSEQUENT TREATMENT?

Advantages of the same clinician doing the initial evaluation and subsequent treatment are as follows:

1. The clinician quickly acquires knowledge about the child, especially if projective techniques have been used.
2. The therapist obtains assessment information directly and not secondhand from the assessor. If another person assesses the child, invariably some knowledge of

the child acquired by the assessor is lost in either oral or written transmission to the therapist.

3. The child does not have to terminate with one adult, the assessor, after the assessment sessions and then start all over with another adult, the therapist. If a positive relationship has built up between the assessor and the child, then the therapy work can begin sooner, since rapport building will not have to be done anew with a different therapist.

4. Parents might feel a better sense of continuity with their clinic contacts when they deal with only one person. They often resent having to "tell their tale" all over again with a new person.

Disadvantages of the same clinician doing the initial evaluation and subsequent treatment are as follows:

1. In the assessment the child learns one mode of interaction with the clinician, namely, sitting still for tests, giving information, keeping attention focused on task, and the like. The assessor will have set up these expectations for the child and perhaps have had to work at enforcing them. If the child begins therapy with the play method, the rules are all changed and there is less structure, less sustained focus, less question-and-answer—in short, less authoritative behavior by the adult. The child may be confused by this. It might be noted, though, that it is much easier for the child to adjust to an adult moving from a more structured and directive rule to a less structured and nondirective rule than vice versa. This is a strong argument for obtaining an assessor different from the therapist if testing is done after therapy is under way.

2. If the therapist uses an existential, nondirective model, then assessment procedures that are directive, intrusive, and not entirely open as to intent would go against the grain for the therapist. Such a therapist, however,

might make use of another clinician's assessment without violating how he/she prefers to relate to the child.

3. If the child or family disagrees with the assessor's conclusions, they may not wish to work further with the assessor but might still be willing to work with another clinician at the same agency.

4. The information gathered from the child during an assessment is generally more widely discussed in psychological reports to parents and outside agencies than is information gathered during therapy. This openness might undermine the level of trust needed for a therapeutic alliance. With different clinicians doing the assessment and the treatment, this potential source of mistrust of the therapist by the child is reduced.

5. The use of another clinician to do the assessment can give the therapist additional information. The assessor and the therapist might see the child's conflicts, problems, feelings, strengths, and development somewhat differently, and these differences could broaden the therapist's understanding. The therapist might have some "blind spots" in viewing the child that could become evident through a thorough assessment. As the therapeutic relationship builds, the therapist in turn may perceive aspects of the child that the assessor missed. The point here is that two heads are better than one.

SHOULD PSYCHODIAGNOSTIC TESTING TAKE PLACE IN A PLAYROOM?

Testing a child in a playroom can present some problems. It may make little difference for the older child (except that the child may feel insulted at having to use the little kid's room) or the younger child who has good impulse control and attention-focusing skills. However, the usual playroom materials might interfere with standard testing procedures. They undoubtedly seem much more interesting than the test materials or the "dumb" test questions. Even if the child resists getting up to play with the material, the tension created in the child by such temptation could depress the child's test performance. If the only room available for testing the child is a playroom, the examiner would avoid potential problems by removing from sight as much of the play material as possible.

In a few cases, however, it may be preferable to use a playroom for psychodiagnostic testing. Sometimes children will not cooperate with the testing when given in the standard manner. The child may have, for example, a strong need to control situations and be unable to tolerate taking another person's direction, or the child might be so angry at the parents for making him/her come to the clinic that he/she refuses to respond to the examiner. In such cases the child might need to proceed on his/her own terms, perhaps giving the examiner test items or leaving the testing situation altogether. In such cases the examiner may slip items into the free play, e.g., building a block bridge (Stanford-Binet, age 3) or introducing the Rorschach plates after making inkblots together or taking turns giving each other words to define. For an excellent presentation of case material illustrating such an approach see Kaplan (1975). In these kinds of cases, it may be desirable to conduct the diagnostic testing in a playroom to allow easy flow between structured and unstructured interactions.

How Can You Effectively Present to the Parents Information about the Child?

The usual occasions when the child clinician gives psychological information to the child's parents are in an interpretive session after the initial assessment period and periodically during the course of psychotherapy. The primary goal of these occasions is, of course, for the parents to receive information that will help them better understand their child. Frequently, a second goal of the clinician is that the parents change their attitude toward and their behavior with the child in order to help the child achieve a better adjustment.

In order to set the stage clearly at the beginning of the interpretive session I often make a comment like, "I ["we" if the evaluation was done by a team] have been collecting all kinds of information from you and Susan; now it is time to reverse the flow. I'll tell you how I see Susan's strengths and difficulties, and you will have a chance to ask the questions. Then hopefully together we can figure out how best to help Susan." Some such statement ought to put the parents in a receptive mood but also let them know that you do not have any magic answers and that you need to work together to find solutions. In fact, it may be helpful to acknowledge the parents' and your wish for easy solutions but that the reality is not so simple; otherwise the parents would not need outside help. It might be useful also to mention that the child's problems were many months or years in the making, and it will take time and much effort to help the child effectively deal with these problems.

The most frequent mistake beginning therapists make in feedback sessions to parents is to give too much information too fast for the parents to absorb. The clinician has had a great deal of time to digest information and construct a picture of the child. To give this in one large piece to the parents may just overload their systems. A strategy that I have found effective for avoiding this is to have in mind three or four of the main points about the child that I then present one at a time. After presenting each point I ask if the parents have seen examples of it. Most often the parents will see the point immediately and come up with several examples. In this way they incorporate what I am saying into their own experiences with the child. On those occasions when they do not see what I am saying about the child, the point needs further exploration. Perhaps the parents have, for their own psychological reasons, a blind spot in that area. Perhaps the child reveals a conflict, an attitude or a feeling only through fantasy seen in the play session or on projective tests, and the parents have never seen it. Perhaps I am wrong about the point or it is a very minor part of the child's overall psychological functioning.

After the first point has been presented and mutually examined by the parent and myself, I present the second point in a like manner. If the session is for feedback to parents after an initial assessment of the child, a written report for the parents can be useful. During one assessment we noted that the parents had great difficulty in hearing what was being said to them, so a written report on the child was prepared to give them during the interpretive hour. Twenty minutes after the feedback session ended I saw them standing in the middle of the sidewalk in front of the clinic deeply absorbed in studying the report. In this day of open records you might consider routinely giving parents jargon-free reports on their child.

After you have conveyed to the parents the essence of how you see the problem, and you and the parents are in basic agreeement as to the nature of the child's problem, then it is time to turn your attention to working out solutions. Since you are the expert, you need to have some alternative interventions in mind to suggest to the parents. The plan that is actually adopted will depend on the intervention alternatives available and the parents' time and psychological and financial resources. Beginning clinicians may not give sufficient weight to these realities in the parents' lives and may become impatient with parents who do not jump at what the clinician considers the ideal treatment plan. The child clinician should, in my view, be a child advocate but also needs to temper the advocate position with the realities of circumstances in the child's life. If the parents sense that the clinician understands their position as well as the child's, then planning together will undoubtedly go much more smoothly. The parents are more likely to follow through with treatment plans they have helped formulate. The paradox here is that if the clinician is a bit less of an overt child advocate, the child may end up getting more.

Sometimes parents simply will not accept your assessment conclusions and recommendations. This might be the case where the child was referred by another agency, such as a school, and the parents felt forced into bringing the child to the clinic. Or perhaps the parents have some hidden agenda, such as wanting their unruly child to be hospitalized, or they might wish their child to be placed in a special program for the gifted or mentally retarded. If you try to convince the parents of the "correctness" of your conclusions and recommendations, the parents will most likely resist even more. So what can you do? It would be most constructive if you could align yourself with the parents as a person who shares their concern about the welfare of their child. You can try talking openly about their concerns and differences of opinion. In the final analysis, however, you are not going to be able to "sell" your recommendations. You can only state what you believe is best for the child and why and then let the parents do what they will.

Chapter 4

FIRST CONTACT

WHAT WOULD YOU ADVISE THE PARENT(S) TO TELL THE CHILD ABOUT COMING TO THE FIRST SESSION?

What the parent tells the child about the clinic prior to the first visit often suggests much about the parent-child relationship. Less than open, straight communication between parent and child would be suggested by the following: the parent blames the child ("We are having to go to the doctor because you are bad"); the parent lies to the child ("We are going to the zoo"); the parent doesn't tell the child anything, just puts the child in the car and drives to the clinic; the parent threatens the child ("If you don't behave, I'll tell the doctor so he won't like you"); and the parent bribes the child ("If you go see the doctor without a fuss, I'll give you an ice cream").

Parents will sometimes ask the child's therapist or the clinic intake worker what they should say to their child prior to the first visit. Even if they do not ask, it may be helpful to give the parents some suggestions as to words they might use with their child to explain coming to the clinic. Whatever is suggested should facilitate clear, honest communication. Here is one example. The parent says, "We are concerned about [your fighting with Judy so much, our hollering and fussing at each other so much of the time, your sadness—whatever the problem is] so we will go see X [the child worker] for some help. X does not use needles [if that indeed is the case]; rather he/she helps kids by talking and playing with them." If the child asks further questions such as: "What will we play with?" "How old is X?" "How long will I go there?" "Will X shrink my head?" and if the parent knows the answers, then he/she should be urged to answer them in a straightforward manner. If the parent does not know the answers, then the child should be encouraged to find out for him/herself when at the clinic.

How Can You Deal with a Child's Resistance to Coming into the Therapy Room?

Every beginning child worker has the fantasy of being left standing at the starting gate. "How can I evaluate or treat the child who refuses to leave Mother in the waiting room?" "What will my supervisor think about me if I can't even get the child into the therapy room?" "Why am I getting into this business anyway?" Quite often the beginning child worker focuses his/her anxiety about all aspects of training in a new profession or a new subspecialty on the question of the resistant child. I tell the students to relax, that the probabilities that they will draw a resistant child for their first case are small. This reassurance, of course, does nothing to lower anxiety.

The refusal of the child to separate from the mother almost always is the result of fear: fear of losing mother, fear of the stranger, fear of an unknown room, or fear of losing autonomy, of being changed against his/her will.

Underlying the fear in each of these instances is the child's perception of possible loss: loss of parent, loss of control, loss of self. The child's refusal to go into the therapy room reveals much about the child's level of fear, about his/her way of dealing with that fear, about the child's relationship with the mother (or other person bringing the child to the clinic), and about the mother's behavior toward the child. The beginning child worker needs to remember that assessment does not begin in the playroom; it begins as soon as the child and mother are first observed.

All of this theoretical discussion will probably not help lower the anxiety of the beginning worker. The response I have frequently received from a student after going over the above points is, "Yes, but what should I *do?*" The following is offered not as *the* way to deal with the reluctant child but as *a* way to respond. Students find that they feel more comfortable if they have in mind some definite steps they can take, even if the actual interchange seldom follows the script they have in mind.

After introducing yourself to the mother you might turn to the child and say, "And you must be [name]." Squat down to the child's level. "How are you? We are going to play some games. Come on, let me show you the playroom." (Be careful not to ask the child a question that may be answered with a yes or no, such as "Do you want to come with me?" If the child answers, "No," then you are stuck; either you accept the child's answer and abort your relationship or you do not accept the no and act contrary to the child's stated desires.) Turn around and head for the door. At the door turn your head to see if the child is following. If not, say, "Come on, let's go." If the child does not come say, "Well, let's have your mom come with us. Come on. Your mother can see where we will be." At the door of the therapy room say, "See, this is where we will be playing, and your mother will be in the waiting room." If the child refuses to separate at this point, simply ask them both into the room and invite the mother to sit in a chair that you have placed near the door. Ask her in a polite way to just remain passive and let you interact with the child at the child's own pace. Invite the child to explore the room. If the child is reluctant to leave the mother, get some materials like clay or paper and crayon or blocks and sit on the floor somewhere in the child's half of the room (do not crowd the child) and begin playing with the materials. Do not push or urge the child; just begin playing and expect that the child will join in. The mother will undoubtedly urge the child to become involved in the play, but just say to her, "It's OK, let him join in when he is ready." If the child eventually joins you in play and you feel the child is quite comfortable, you might ask the mother if she would just step out to the waiting room and wait there until you and the child are finished playing.

If the child still refuses to separate after a session or two of the above routine, then indeed you have an interesting mother-child relationship.

Chapter 5

ESTABLISHING AND MAINTAINING A RELATIONSHIP WITH THE CHILD

WHAT ARE SOME INITIAL MOVES YOU CAN MAKE TO START A RELATIONSHIP?

The general answer to this question is to act naturally with the child. Don't be condescending. As children we have all been put off by the neighbor or distant relative who said to us in a falsetto voice, "My, what a big boy you are!" or "Aren't you a pretty little girl!" Also to be avoided are the stock questions: "How old are you?" "What school do you go to?" "What grade are you in?" "What is your favorite subject?" "What do you want to be when you grow up?" "Do you have any brothers or sisters?" These are some of the approaches that do not help establish rapport with a child. What does help?

The first contact probably will be in the waiting room. You might approach the adult with the child and say, "Are you Mrs. [Smith]?" If she indicates yes, say, "Hello, I'm [Joe Dodds]." Turn to the child and say, "And you must be [Michael]. Come on [Michael], I want to show you the playroom." In a recent first encounter with an 8-year-old client, Scott, I had a parking sticker from the clinic office for the parent's car. I explained to Scott how it needed to be stuck on the window so they would not get a parking ticket and asked him if he would mind going out to put it on the inside of the rear window. Scott soon returned saying that the Scotch tape I had put on the sticker was on the wrong side for the sticker to show through the window, which caused laughter all around. This episode accomplished several things by way of establishing a beginning relationship between Scott and me. It was a real task that needed doing, and I let Scott know that I believed he was competent to do the job and independent enough to achieve it. It was a reasonable request for help that established the link between two people—"You have done something for me so you may expect that I shall try to do something for you." My error with the tape and laughing at myself gave the message to Scott that this doctor is human and he does not pretend to be infallible.

On the way to the playroom it would be natural to make small talk such as casually saying, "Have you been here before?" "You are probably wondering what it is like here." "I like that sweater you are wearing." Or even a weather comment like "What do you think of all this snow?"

On entering the therapy room you might say, "Here is where we will be working and playing together." If you then stand around awkwardly, the child is likely to feel your discomfort, which will add to the child's own anxiety. Do something that feels natural, such as sitting on the floor or wandering over to pick up a ball or a piece of clay to fiddle with. This activity should not be the focus of your interest; rather the child should be. You will be modeling the combination of play and talk. You may wish to tell the child that he/she can look the room over and allow some time for exploration.

Within the opening minutes of the first session, I pre-

fer to tell the child openly and simply what I know about
him/her, what my understanding is of the presenting
problem that brought the child to the clinic, and how we
will work together. Here is an example of how it might go:
"Jay, let me ask you, what is the reason your parents
brought you here?" Seldom will children at this early stage
reveal to the therapist, even if they know, the reasons they
were brought to the clinic. Usually children will say, "I don't
know", or give some peripheral reason. Continue with,
"Well, let me tell you how I understand it; then you can
tell me how you see it. Your mother has told me that she
is very worried about your fighting so much at school and
that you are upset sometimes about your father leaving
home last year. Did you know she worried about that? She
doesn't like you to be so unhappy, so she came here for
some help. I told her that I couldn't make you stop fighting
at school, but after we got to know each other, I would try
to understand what was going on from your point of view
and be of help to you if I could. But first we have to get
to know each other, and that is what this room is set up
for. I am always a little nervous when I first meet someone,
so let's play today. Why don't you look around and see
what you want to do?"

   In the long run, I believe, it is easiest to let the child
know immediately what you know about the reason for the
referral. If you wait for the child to bring up the referral
issue, it may never come up. Some nondirective therapists,
such as existentialist Clark Moustakas, would argue that
one should be truly nondirective, and that if the child does
not introduce a topic, then he/she is not ready to deal with
it. To spend so much time with a child waiting for him/
her to bring up a psychologically important topic produces
much tension in the therapist and must influence the therapist's interaction with the child. I believe that telling the
child straight out what you know clears the air and helps

set the stage for open communication by modeling openness early in the relationship. Of course, the child does not
have to plunge right into a discussion of the problem if
he/she is not ready to do so, which is the usual case, but
at least the door has been unlocked.

One of the first techniques students in basic adult in-
terviewing usually learn is to ask open rather than closed
questions that can be answered by yes, no, or other single
words. This is also a good technique in relating to children.
For example, asking, "What do you like to do for fun with
your friends?" has far greater potential for establishing
continuing interaction than does "Do you have many
friends?" or even "Who are your friends?" The temptation
to ask yes-no questions is particularly great with children
who are not very fluent in their initial dialogue—at least
you get *some* response. The problem is that the conversation
quickly takes on the tone of a grilling. It is probably best
to stop asking questions entirely than to fall into this pattern. Of course, the advantage in working with a child in
a playroom as compared to an adult in an interview room
is that you do have materials on which you can focus your
mutual attention; asking no questions at all is an alternative
to asking closed questions when the child is not responding
to open questions.

In some clinics the intake interview is with the entire
family. In my experience, family intake opens up a great
deal of material very quickly and is also valuable in learning
about family feelings and dynamics. The family intake also
affords an excellent way for the therapist to establish immediate rapport with the late-latency-age child or adolescent. Generally, the parents have one worker and the identified child client another. If the family session is followed
by an individual session where you will be alone with the
child for the first time, a good entree to forming an alliance
with the child is to start by commenting on the vibrations

you picked up in the family session. You might say something like "Boy, that was a heavy session! It felt like the whole blame was being dumped on you." or "Wow! I was sure uncomfortable in there; there sure was a lot of anger flying around." In my experience such comments give the child an immediate sense of alliance with the therapist. The child thinks, "Here is someone who knows what it is like for me in my family."

How Do You Get on the Child's Level?

To be in the child therapy business, it helps to be able to regress in one's level of play. If you feel terribly awkward and uncomfortable sitting on the floor playing with dolls in a dollhouse or engaging in silly rhyming games with a child, then you should think twice about becoming a child therapist. For the effective child therapist the regression is not total; although the therapist interacts at the child's level, one corner of the therapist's mind is aware of the regression, monitoring what is transpiring, and speculating about the meaning the play has for the child.

Being loose and a bit goofy in the playroom could be helpful to both inhibited and impulse-ridden children. For the inhibited, too-grown-up child, the regressive behavior of the therapist can model for the child that it is safe to act in an immature way, that one does not become permanently regressed but can act older when the play time is over. For the impulsive child, the therapist's regressive behavior can model controlled regression, that is, acting out infantile impulses without losing control. Such play with this type of child often progresses with the therapist continually reminding the child of the limits on wild behavior.

A practical suggestion as to how to get on the child's level is to literally, physically, get on the child's eye level.

This means dressing in clothes that allow comfortable floor sitting. At the very least, the therapist should sit on a child-size chair. When the therapist is on the child's physical level, then he/she can follow and amplify the child's lead in play. For example, if the child makes two dolls fight, the therapist can provide sound effects; if the mother doll spanks the child doll, the therapist can cry for the child; if the child squashes a ball of clay, the therapist can squash a ball even more vigorously.

How Directive Should You Be?

The answer to this question depends entirely on the therapist's theoretical model. The existential therapist assumes that regenerative forces lie predominantly within the child and that, given the proper climate, the child will achieve a more complex and adaptive level of dealing with stresses. Therefore, the existential therapist would be nondirective. If the goal is to teach the child new skills or to modify the child's behavior in some way, then the behavior therapist would, of course, be quite directive. Somewhere in between these two points on the directiveness dimension would be the psychoanalytically oriented psychotherapist whose objective is to focus on and bring to consciousness material from the unconscious, so as to allow resolution of neurotic conflicts. In the psychoanalytic sessions the child is allowed free play with flexible materials, but the therapist picks up on symbolically significant play and play productions. The therapist encourages further elaboration of the play, probes as to its meaning for the child, and perhaps interprets to the child the significance of what is revealed through the play.

Also, between the two extremes of directive-nondirective are models that allow for a shift during any one session in the degree of directivenes. These models employ periodic teaching of the child within a generally nondirective framework. Examples of such teaching are helping the child achieve cognitive comprehension of conflicting emotions (Harter 1977) or teaching an isolated child how he/she turns off other children by pointing out how he/she annoys the therapist. It is in the spirit of the therapist accepting what the child has to offer that the child, one hopes, will accept what the therapist offers from time to time.

We know enough about nonverbal, subtle reinforcement in a two-person system to know that truly nondirective therapy is impossible. What the successful nondirective child therapist should be doing is behaving in ways that reinforce a child's self-expression. Reinforcing behaviors of the therapist could include giving attention, smiling, joining in the play by following the child's lead, and so on. The child may express him/herself by making choices, by creating products (tangible and fantasy), and by examining his/her behavior and desires. By paying close attention to the child's explorations and products the therapist also conveys the message to the child that he/she highly values the child as a unique individual. The nondirective therapist becomes directive, however, when the child crosses or threatens to cross the limits of the therapy situation by harming self, therapist, or room.

In reality few, if any, therapists are entirely consistent in the degree of control or direction they assume during any one session or from session to session. Whatever the therapist's theoretical orientation, the skilled worker responds to the child's needs, moods, and behavior and to his/her own needs and moods in a flexible way to maintain rapport and balance in their working relationship. Allowing the child some latitude of behavior and a good measure of control of the therapy situation helps maintain the child's interest and motivation for continuing therapy work.

How Do You Deal with Questions the Child Asks about Your Personal Life?

In tackling this question it is helpful to distinguish be-tween two variables that are not necessarily related: degree of openness of the therapist within the therapy relationship and degree of revelation to the client of the therapist's life outside the therapy relationship. For an excellent discussion of this issue, see Jourard (1971). These two variables are represented graphically in Figure 5–1. The open-closed variable has to do with how real, how emotionally respon-sive the therapist is with the child, how much the therapist shares his/her reactions in the relationship with the child. The privacy variable is just what the label says: how much of the therapist's life outside the therapy relationship is revealed to the child? In Figure 5–1, therapist X is open in expressing feelings to the client about their relationship. Much of the time she reveals to the client when she is hap-py, angry, excited, or sad about the client's behavior, ideas, feelings, and experiences and about the therapy relation-ship. She also reveals a great deal of her private life—her family and other relationships and her experiences outside the therapy room. Therapist Y is even more open in her relationship with her client but reveals very little about her life outside of the therapy relationship. You may place yourself in any position on this graph to represent how open you choose to be in your relationship with your client and about your life outside the therapy relationship. Your position on the privacy dimension may be anywhere from telling the child nothing about your private life, to simply answering questions but not elaborating, to sharing prac-tically everything and introducing private material into the session even when the child has not asked about it.

Whatever you decide about how much of your per-sonal life you will disclose to the child, most children in therapy become curious and sooner or later ask about their

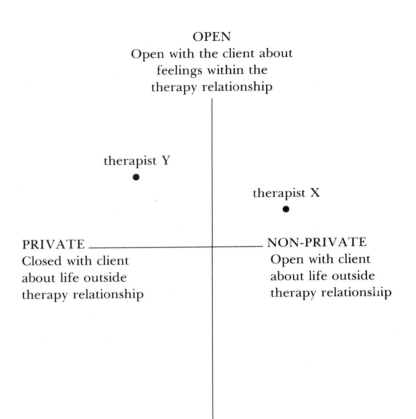

Figure 5–1. Two dimensions of openness: therapist's private life and therapist's relationship with the client.

therapist's life outside the therapy hour. "Are you married?" "Do you have any children?" "What is your house like?" "Do you have any pets?" "Do you see other children here?" These questions, of course, grow from the child's need to figure out the relationship between him/herself and the therapist. Jealousy is often an issue. The child might think, "Am I so important as to be the only thing of importance in your life?"

How might you respond to a child's questions about your children, for example, if you are open about yourself in therapy but closed in revealing information about your private life? Here are some possibilities: "Why do you ask?" "I'm flattered you are interested in me enough to ask." "You must be very curious about my life outside this room." If the child persists in wanting to know the answer to the question, you might say something like: "I have a rule against talking about myself, what I do, outside of this hour. What is the most important thing is you and me right here, right now in this room." If the child responds with disappointment or anger you might say, "I feel bad [said only if you really feel bad] about not being able to tell you because I know you really want to know, and I don't like to disappoint you."

It is often informative to find out what the child's fantasies about you are. They could reveal something about the child's wishes and fears regarding the relationship with you. Even if you do answer the child's questions, say, about whether you have children, you might say, "I will tell you, but first let's see what you think; do you think I have children?" If, however, you have taken the position that you will not tell the child whether you have children or not, then it is probably better not to engage in this dialogue, because it would be too provocative to the child and too withholding on your part.

You may wish to pursue with the child his/her feelings that led to the question and about the frustration of receiving no answer. In any case, if you are open in your relationship, you say how you feel about the child's asking the personal question and how you feel about being pressed for an answer. In other words, you may be very open about your emotional reactions and feelings in that situation but still not reveal anything about your private life.

How Do You Get to a Feeling Level in the Relationship?

Implied in this question is an unstated value that working on the feeling level with a child in therapy is desirable. I hold that value. There is nothing sacrosanct about dealing with feelings per se, but most of the children with whom we use play therapy techniques come to us with difficulties in the emotional-behavioral sphere. They may also have cognitive deficits, but if these are the primary reason for referral, reeducational techniques are generally used to help the child. The kinds of emotional difficulties children who are referred to child therapists often have are too much guilt, too much anger, too much sadness, and conflicts between incompatible emotions. The psychodymic theories hold that these problems may result in maladaptive behavior and that one way to change behavior is to have the children learn to identify their feelings cognitively and change them or learn to deal with them in more adaptive ways. This is not to imply that cognitive and educational techniques cannot be used to help understand and change behavior but rather that the emphasis in this kind of therapy is on the emotions.

The therapist has two general approaches to getting on a feeling level with children: modeling feelings that the therapist is having or has had and labeling and encouraging the expression of the child's feelings. The first step for the therapist who wishes to model the expression of feelings is to identify and monitor his/her own feelings as well as those of the child. Self-disclosure begets self-disclosure, as Sidney Jourad's (1971) research has demonstrated. The therapist can then model the expression of feelings by making comments such as, "Whoopee! I am glad when I win a game." "I don't like to lose, I feel stupid [or angry]." Or "I am getting bored with this game." Clearly the therapist does not keep a running commentary that reflects the continual parade of feelings being experienced, but he/she selects those feelings that are strongest or, more importantly, those that parallel the feelings the child might be having difficulty admitting or coping with.

Another way the therapist may use his/her own feelings to help the child recognize feelings is to reflect how the therapist feels (or has felt) in a situation similar to that being experienced or described by the child. For example, "I get really upset with myself when I can't hit the target." "That is interesting that you were not upset when you got the F's on your report card, because I used to get terribly sad when I got poor grades. I thought I was really stupid." Or "I used to get furious with my mother when she made me come in from playing to watch my baby brother." The therapist, however, must be truthful in these statements or the child will sense their nongenuine nature. Or as the child describes an event in his/her life the therapist might say, "That makes me feel____just to hear about it." With this approach the therapist and child do not get into a conflict around denied feelings; the child can either agree with or ignore the statement, since how the therapist would feel is not debatable by the child. Possibly a responsive chord will be struck in the child like, "Hey, this old person is human; he [she] really understands me." Even if the reaction of the therapist does not strike a similar emotional chord in the child, the child might at least feel, "Well, he [she] is wrong but is trying to understand me anyhow. I must be worth trying for."

In addition to modeling the verbal expression of feeling, the therapist can label the child's feelings for him/her. It is easy, however, to overdo this, and I have had children tell me to shut up about feelings. One of my students was working with a child who was particularly closed to his feelings. Whenever the therapist tried to talk about feelings or interpersonal events, the child would say something like "Shut up, you're wasting our time. Don't talk, play!" Occasional casual comments might help the child learn to label; e.g., "You seem mad today," or "Let's celebrate your happy feeling." Questions can be used, such as "I should imagine you would be jealous of your sister. Are you?"

Cognitive devices, like having children draw conflicting feelings in one person, can be very helpful. See S. Harter (1977, 1982) for an excellent discussion of this device and the rationale behind it. With younger children I have occasionally used a series of faces drawn to depict different emotions, asking the child to point to the one most nearly like his/her feeling.

To move beyond simply becoming aware of, labeling, and/or expressing feelings the therapist, through discussion or simple illustration, can help the child learn (a) acceptance of his/her feelings, (b) reasons underlying the feelings, and (c) ways to cope with emotions that result in more satisfactory interpersonal relationships for the child. The level of these discussions must be geared to the level of the child's language development, cognitive development, and tolerance for dealing with generally upsetting feelings. Beginning therapists frequently hold too high expectations for these kinds of conversations with child clients, tending to want the child therapy to be a minature form of adult psychotherapy. This verbal level of emotional work with children is often slow and frequently impossible.

As a rule, it is generally best to stick with the child's metaphor. That is, if the child is projecting a current family conflict and his/her own feelings into a doll play scene, the therapist does not explicitly relate the play scenario to the child's life at home; rather, the therapist encourages the child to develop the play as a means of expressing feelings, conflicts, and attitudes. In this way the child will bring feelings into consciousness only to the extent that he/she is able to tolerate owning these feelings.

WHEN AND HOW DO YOU START INTERPRETING TO THE CHILD?

We need first to define interpreting, then see which theoretical orientations do and do not call for interpreting, and finally, explore some techniques for interpreting.

In psychotherapy, interpreting means the therapist brings into the client's awareness feelings, attitudes, and relationships between events in the client's life of which he/she had been unaware. The levels of interpreting might be described as (a) identifying and labeling feelings in the client, (b) identifying sources of feelings, and (c) connecting past events in the client's life with current feelings, thoughts, and behaviors.

The child therapist working within the behavioral model may not interpret at all but rather work on changing overt behaviors. He/she might identify thoughts and feelings (responses) and interpret to the child their source (stimulus) if the thoughts or feelings were targeted for change. If the behavior therapist connected past events in the child's life with current feelings, thoughts, and behaviors, it would be called establishing a learning history.

The existential therapist, being nondirective, would not interpret at all but would provide a safe, accepting environment and wait for the child to experience repressed thoughts, feelings, and connections whenever the child could comfortably tolerate awareness of them.

Both the cognitive therapist and the psychodynamic therapist, for all their differences, would probably interpret at all three levels. Both would assume that the purpose of bringing thoughts and feelings into awareness is to help the child gain control and deal more adaptively with them. That this assumption has been challenged for lack of evidence has not stopped the cognitive or psychodynamic therapist from interpreting.

Preadolescent children often do not have concepts to understand psychodynamic interpretations such as unconscious motives, why they are a threat, and how defenses operate to keep them out of awareness (Harter 1982). If interpretations are made to a child, it is difficult to know whether they hit the mark, that is, whether they are in fact about material in the child's unconscious and whether the child is now aware of that material. Further, it is not known if bringing material to the child's consciousness makes any difference in the child's feelings and attitudes, since the child may lack the conceptual and verbal ability to express any changes to the therapist. Often the only indication of the therapist's accuracy in making an interpretation is a change in the child's behavior.

When in the course of play therapy do you start interpreting? If the model you are using calls for interpreting to the child, then you do so whenever you know what you are talking about and the child is able to "hear" the interpretation. Probably your relationship with the child will have gone on long enough for you to have become well acquainted with each other, first, so that you know the child well enough that you have evidence for the validity of the interpretations you make to the child, and second, so that the child knows and trusts you well enough that he/she may pay some attention to what you are saying. Interpretations would be given sparingly, since you are unlikely to come up with 15 valid interpretations in a session, and even if you did, the child would probably think you were weird with all your talk. Beginning therapists often worry about giving the wrong interpretation. In my opinion a wrong interpretation offered in a speculative manner to the child will not do any harm because the child will not accept what does not fit. This is especially true if the interpretation is made in an indirect manner, as discussed below.

How do you make interpretations to a child? Unless the child is in his/her teens and is really verbal, it is doubtful if verbal modality can be used effectively to make interpretations to the child. The techniques of interpreting to a child will vary according to the child's conceptual capacities and psychological readiness to hear interpretations. Susan Harter (1982) has beautifully described four levels of techniques of interpreting, from the least direct to the most direct. The *first level* she describes is interpreting through a doll play scenario by making an interpretation about a doll that resembles the child in some respect. For example, you might say, "This boy [doll] is shoplifting because he is angry at his father for leaving the family." The *second level* is to make an interpretation about a doll, as in level one, then to make a link between the doll character and the child: "I wonder if you feel like this boy sometimes." The *third level* is to make an indirect interpretation by discussing a "friend" who is like your client. You might say to your 9-year-old, red-haired client, "I have this friend who is nine years old and has red hair who, whenever he gets really angry at his father, goes out and steals something." Though the technique is transparent to the child, it does give the child a bit of distance or a chance to say, "Well, I'm not like *that* friend." Finally, the *fourth level* is direct verbal interpretation to the child. For a more detailed explanation and rationale of these levels I urge you to read this excellent work of Harter's (1982).

Chapter 6

CONFIDENTIALITY

What Do You Tell the Child about Being Taped or Observed?

Some feel that in this electronic age personal privacy is in danger of being completely eroded. Orwell's *1984* is at hand. Those who feel strongly about this might argue that observation by unseen and unknown persons through one-way glass and electronic devices can *never* be justified. Observation and recording can, however, be extremely valuable for training purposes (students observing senior clinicians, either directly or on tape, and supervisors observing supervisees' work). In addition to these uses many clinicians, myself included, have found videotape a useful medium for having a family see themselves in action in order to help them understand and change interactions within the family. I feel that the potential benefits of taping and observing child psychotherapy outweigh the erosion of privacy *if* each of the following conditions is met: (a) telling the child at the beginning of the session or, if possible, at the previous session, that you are planning to tape or have observers; (b) telling the child the purpose of taping or observation, including who will and who will not have access to it; (c) showing the child how the machinery works; (d) introducing the observers and/or camera operators to the child; and (e) asking the child's permission for the taping or observation to proceed.

One could argue that what the child does not know will not hurt him/her, but ethical principles aside, that stance has a serious danger. If the child learns by some accident midway in the session that he/she is being observed, the child's trust in the therapist could be shattered beyond repair. Thus, it is safer to tell the child of your plans for taping or observing at the very beginning of the session. Of course such knowledge changes the behavior of the child and the therapist, sometimes very little but sometimes a great deal. The argument that the child's knowledge of being observed spoils his/her natural behavior is fallacious, since there is nothing natural in the child therapy setup anyhow. Finally, most psychologists agree that spying on people without their awareness is simply unethical (see APA Ethical Standards).

It is probably easier not to record or have observers at the first session because too many new things are happening too fast and the relationship between therapist and child is too tentative to start right off with the business of explaining the observations, introducing the observers, and securing the child's permission. As the child encounters the one-way glass in his/her explorations of the playroom, I explain what it is and take the child to the other side to see how it works and to show that no one is watching. If, in fact, there were someone observing, I would not wait for the child to discover the observer but would have gone through the steps outlined in the first paragraph.

If taping and observing are used solely for training purposes, then the child's relatives, teachers, or friends will not have access to the sessions. This should be made clear to the child, since unknown trainees and supervisors would probably present less of a threat to the child's sense of privacy than would significant people in the child's life.

Most children of any talking age are interested in how one-way glass and the video system work. Letting the child turn the lights off and on for the one-way glass or see him/herself on TV is fun and helps remove some of the mystery of these devices. The child also gains a bit of a sense of control that could be important to the child who generally feels powerless. Introducing the child to the observer(s) and/or camera operator(s) both removes the mystery of the unknown observer and demonstrates to the child that he/she is not being observed by anyone the child knows.

I generally comment to the child that being taped or observed makes me a bit nervous at first but that I usually get used to it and that probably the same will be true for the child. However, I continue, if the taping or observing makes the child too upset, then it will be stopped. If the therapist takes this final step of securing the child's permission, it will help safeguard against an unwanted invasion of the child's privacy. However, the therapist must be prepared to accept the consequences of the child's "stop" decision, which is that one cannot absolutely count on using the tape or observation for teaching or supervision purposes.

How Much of What You Learn about the Child Should You Reveal and to Whom: Child, Parents, Supervisor, Authorities?

The simplest answer to this question would be to reveal nothing about the child to anybody. If this principle is stated to and demonstrated to the child, a climate of trust and openness between child and therapist should be established in the shortest order. However, the position of the absolutely closed child-therapist system is legitimately assailed from many quarters. The commonly accepted violation of the confidentiality between a therapist and an adult client occurs when someone's life is in danger, usually a threat of suicide or murder. The same principle should apply to the child client-therapist relationship. That is, outside help would be sought if the child were threatening suicide, murder, or the undertaking of a venture that would be hazardous to someone's safety. When applying this simple exception principle, however, gray areas are soon encounterd. What would you do, for example, if you learned that your 11-year-old client was planning to take an unknown dose of Quaaludes? Would you watch him/her play chemical roulette? What would you do if your child client told you he/she was planning to run away? Do you say something if you suspect your child is being abused? These latter two issues are discussed further in Chapter 9.

The child's therapist or the clinic where the therapist works is generally not the agent of the child. The psychologist who works for the court or the school or the parent is the agent of the court, school, or parent. These contractors have some legitimate claim to information from the therapist about the child.

Therapists who see children in a training clinic are obliged, for the sake of teaching and learning, to reveal information about a child and the process of therapy to the trainers or the trainees. Most of these clinics explain the educational nature of the clinic and the client or client's agent (e.g., parent) signs a waiver giving permission for recording and observing the therapy sessions. In this case the clinic as whole could be considered the therapist, and confidentiality is held between client and clinic.

Through a phone call from a teacher or through a whispered contact from the parent in the waiting room, the therapist might learn something about the child such as some recent (usually "bad") behavior. Is the therapist then under any obligation to tell the child what was just learned? Certainly, if the therapist were modeling openness of communication, the pressure would be high to do so. If the therapist models openness in communication from parent to therapist to child, wouldn't the child expect the communication to flow freely in the opposite direction also?

In the face of these and other pressures, it is tempting to view seriously the other end of the confidentiality spectrum and keep *no* secrets from anybody. In fact, this position characterizes many children's experiences with adults: mothers who tell fathers, teachers who tell mothers, neighbors who tell parents, and so on. From such experiences the child has learned *not* to expose vulnerable areas either to others or to the self. But for therapy to achieve the goal of helping the child feel secure enough to open up intrapsychic areas for exploration and change, such a nonconfidential relationship would be counterproductive.

So what do you do? I will offer here the position I have come to take, recognizing that any position is arbitrary and will neither completely safeguard the confidentiality between therapist and child nor allow for complete revelation of therapy process and content to anyone who asks.

If you gave the whole load to the child at once you might say something like, "What we do and say in here remains private between you and me, unless I learn that you are going to really hurt yourself or someone else. Then I will try to stop you, and I will obtain help from others in doing so. Your mother and father will want to know how you are getting along here. I will not tell them any specific secrets I learn from you but will give them very general statements. In any case, I will tell you first what I plan to say to them and see if that is OK with you. You could even sit in on the session I have with your parents if you wish. The same thing is true with your teachers [and other agencies with a vested interest in the child]. I will tell you what I plan to say and get your reaction. Also, we are being observed by some of my students. They are interested in how I work and will be watching me more than you. You won't ever be observed by anyone you know; I'll introduce you to whoever is observing each time. Then too we are making a videotape of these sessions so I can use it for teaching another group of students. If being observed or taped makes you too nervous, we can stop it, but it will really help out the students here who are learning to work with children. Oh, by the way, I have a supervisor with whom I will be talking about our sessions."

You should be laughing by now. No child is going to comprehend this speech, and if he/she did, he/she would think you were crazy to talk about confidentiality with all those exceptions. The child will understand one element at a time and will build trust in you more through your actions than your words. At the first session you might make the point about private time between you and the child. If the session is observed or taped, introduce that to the child at that time, as discussed above. Before a conference with the parent comes up, you explain that part to the child. In other words, small doses of explanation are needed, and your demonstration of keeping confidence within the limits defined to the child will be the way in which the child may start building trust in you enough to begin revealing psychologically significant material. Complete, unconditional trust should not be expected, since there are realistic limits to preserving complete confidentiality.

What do you tell the child about him/herself? There are two sources of information you have about the child: from your observations (including perhaps assessment material from the initial and subsequent evaluations) and from the parent, teacher, or other persons in the child's life. Information and conclusions you have about the child should be imparted to the child from time to time in my opinion. I have found the natural occasion for giving my opinions to the child is when telling the child the summary statements I plan to give, with the child's permission, to the parent or teacher in progress-reporting conferences.

The material the therapist knows about the child from the referring problem or from the parent, teacher, or other adult should be told to the child immediately. If the therapist seeks out further information, the child might feel as if he/she were being checked up on. I discourage the parent from calling between sessions and reporting on the child's recent behavior, but if the parent does so (there are times when the therapist needs to be advised of *major* events in the child's life), I inform the parents that I will tell the child what was just learned. At the beginning of the next session the information may be introduced with a statement such as "Your mother called me and was really upset about your having skipped school. I told her that I couldn't make you go to school, and wouldn't even if I could, but that I'd let you know she called. If you want to talk about it, fine, but if not, that is OK too. I'm just sorry it is such a hassle for you."

In conclusion, I take the position that the therapist establishes the realities of confidentiality and its limitations a step at a time. The child's growing attachment to the therapist and feeling of trust that the therapist will not indiscriminately reveal psychologically significant and perhaps painful material will develop slowly out of the child's experiences with the therapist's actions, not words. I believe that introducing exceptions to the confidentiality of the child-therapist relationship should be done as the occasion for revealing information about the child arises and should be done with the child's permission, if possible, or at least his/her knowledge of what will be revealed, to whom and why. Such exceptions to keeping strict confidence will necessarily slow down the establishment of trust the child has in the therapist but that is a condition of the realities of therapy with which the child and the therapist must live.

How Do You Answer the Child Who Asks if He/She Can Tell the Content of the Sessions to Someone?

If the child really wants to tell his/her parents or anyone else what goes on in the therapy sessions, that should be the child's right. In any case, the therapist can do little to prevent it except with psychological pressure of some kind on the child, which the child certainly does not need.

How Do You Help a Child Deal with Pressures from Parents to Reveal What Happens in a Therapy Session?

There are many reasons why parents may pressure the child to tell the contents of the therapy session. The parents may simply be curious or there may be one or more of the following motives: protectiveness of their child, jealousy of the special attention and nurture the child is receiving, jealousy of the parental role that they feel is being usurped by the therapist, need to control the life of their child, fear of the child's growing independence from them, or the belief that children should have no secrets from their parents. At the time the treatment plan is made with the parents, when the goals and techniques of therapy are explained to them, the therapist should include an explanation of the confidential nature of the therapy relationship. The explanation might run something like "One of the goals of my work with Helen will be to help her discover some of the things that are bothering her. Children, and we adults too for that matter, often keep things bottled up inside because they are too painful to talk about or even think about. As she comes to feel comfortable with and trust me, she might begin to explore some of those sensitive areas. Of course you will be curious about what is going on in our sessions and will want to ask here about it. If she doesn't volunteer to tell you about these things, it is probably best not to persist in asking her because that will just be one more pressure on her that she does not need."

You might then go on to tell the parents what you plan to tell the child as to your understanding of the presenting problem. Also, this is a good time to discourage frequent reports from the parents on the child's behavior at home, with the proviso that you will be having periodic progress meetings with them, possibly with the child present.

But what if the parents persist in pressuring the child to reveal the contents of the therapy sessions? First, the parents should be helped by whoever is working with them to understand the motives behind their persistent need to know, to understand the pressures this creates for their child, and finally (one hopes), to change their behavior and cease asking the child to tell all.

Second, the child may be helped by two general approaches: understanding the parents' need to know and learning some general responses that could be used in answer to the parents' questions. It is inadvisable to tell the child to refuse to tell the parents what happens in the sessions because few children can stand up to their parents with a flat refusal, and your encouraging the child to do so places him/her in the middle of a direct conflict between your wishes and the parents'. However, the child probably already knows how to be evasive; remember that wonderful book title, *"Where did you go?" "Out." "What did you do?" "Nothing."*?

Here are some words the therapist might use with the child. "I understand that your parents keep asking you to tell them what we do in here. Of course you can tell them if you want to, but if you don't, then that must really put pressure on you. I wonder why they persist so in asking. Naturally, they are curious, but maybe also they think their children should have no secrets from them. Maybe they are jealous of the time we spend together. In any case, I guess they have their reasons. As far as I'm concerned, you don't have to tell them anything, but that is probably hard to say directly to your parents. Perhaps you could just give them general answers like 'We just talked—about stuff' or perhaps you could tell them some of the unimportant stuff and skip the really private things we do and talk about." Naturally you would not give this speech in toto, but it may contain some useful notions if they fit your particular situation. In general, it would be best for the child if the therapist did not cross that very thin line between helping the child cope with parental pressure and giving the child the notion that the therapist is trying to pressure him/her not to tell what happens in therapy.

Chapter 7

PARENTS

WHAT IS THE NATURE OF THE RELATIONSHIP BETWEEN THE CHILD'S THERAPIST AND THE CHILD'S PARENTS?

Parents are important in child psychotherapy. In therapy sessions with the therapist, the child should be changing: learning about self, developing more mature ways of dealing with stress, acquiring new competencies, improving self-image, and achieving greater independence. However, the child does not live only in the therapy room (weekly therapy sessions occupy about six-tenths of 1 percent of the child's time), and the parents play an active part in this change process. Their influence on the change may be positive, negative, or mixed. The ideal relationship between parent and therapist will be described; then some realities will be discussed.

Ideally, the parents, the therapist, and the child all work together to alleviate whatever is presenting a problem for the child and the family. This means arriving at a common view of the problem and its causes plus coming to agreement about the best strategies to be used by each to help resolve the problem. To achieve this close working relationship requires frequent and clear communication between parents, therapist, and child. In a clinic that uses the team approach the parents may be regularly seeing a mental health worker other than the child's therapist. In that case the parents' worker must also establish clear communication with all parties. Yet the privacy of each member of the family would be preserved.

There are many factors both in the family, in the clinicians, and in the nature of the therapeutic enterprise that work against such an ideal relationship. The parents may not be in agreement with each other about the nature of the problem in their family or the decision to seek outside help. A common, though by no means universal, attitude in families is the father's belief that there is no problem or, if there is, that the mother should take care of it since she has primary responsibility for raising the children. The mother may feel that the father is uninvolved with the children and insensitive to both their and her needs. Even if the parents are in agreement about the problem, they may disagree with the clinician's view of the problem and his/her suggestions as to what might be done about it. Often the parents bring the child to the mental health clinic with the same expectation with which they bring the child to a medical clinic, namely, that the doctor should diagnose and treat their child directly, with pills if possible. If the parents are to be involved at all, it is simply to carry out the doctor's instructions at home. This mental set seems counter to the message they usually receive from the mental health clinic personnel, who believe that the parents are an integral part of the problem and that the solutions to the problem lie within the family, individually and collectively. The parents with this attitude would be particularly impatient with play techniques, which they might see as slow in bringing about change. They wonder how "just playing" can help, since the child can play at home and at a much cheaper price!

Sometimes parents bring their child to a mental health clinic as an entree to seeking treatment for themselves, either individually or for their marriage relationship. The clinician should be alert to this possibility and realize that although the parents may be seeking help for themselves, this does not necessarily mean that they do not also want help for their child.

Sometimes parents feel much guilt about "causing" their child's problems. They may react to suggestions from the mental health worker about what they might try in order to alter an impasse with their child as if they were being blamed for that impasse. I have found that a good approach to helping the parents deal with their guilt about causing their child's problem is as follows. If, after a discussion with the parents about the staff's assessment of the problem, usually in the interpretive session, the parents indicate some guilt, the therapist says, "Of course you played an important part in your child's development; he did not grow up in a vacuum. But it is not as if you *deliberately* set out to produce this problem. As your child was growing, you did what you thought was best for him. There was no way for you to anticipate what would happen. Different children react in different ways, and he could have developed quite differently even if you behaved in much the same way. In other words, while you are intimately involved in your child's development, he brings his own characteristics and temperament. No one can blame you for consciously producing problems for your child; certainly you shouldn't blame yourself." (In those rare cases where parents *have* deliberately sabotaged their child's healthy development, they usually do not have *enough* guilt.)

Parents may come to the clinic with much anger at their child for causing stress in the family and for causing the inconvenience and expense of psychotherapy. If this anger is suppressed or repressed, it could make a barrier to open communication between mental health worker and parent.

At least one family therapist, Raymond Pittmen, is convinced that people who seek help at a mental health clinic *do not want to change*. They want to stop hurting, but they want *others* to change. Such an attitude would clearly interfere with communication of suggestions from the mental health worker about steps the parent might try to break the impasse in their family. For many parents the change process in their child might cause them to become frustrated and angry at the clinic. The change is usually slower than the parents would hope for, and sometimes the child's behavior at home becomes even worse! This is particularly true of overly inhibited children who, as therapy progresses, are helped to become more openly expressive. The parents come to the clinic with the half serious plea, "Please put him back the way he was!" In any case the parents might perceive that the child's therapist is allied with the child against them, which would arouse resentment and anger in their struggle to resist change in themselves.

Jealousy of the therapist is experienced by many parents and can certainly interfere with a close, cooperative working relationship between parents and clinic staff. The jealousy of any one parent has several potential sources. The parent with high dependency needs might be jealous of the exclusive attention the child receives in the close therapeutic relationship. The parent who feels inadequate as a parent (probably this feeling is true of the majority of parents who seek mental health help) might believe that the child's therapist makes a better parent than he/she does and therefore becomes jealous of the therapist.

Before we condemn parents too readily or too severely, let us remind ourselves that not all of the factors disruptive to good communication and working relationships between mental health workers and parents lie on the parents' side; the child's therapist is also liable to have some destructive attitudes and feelings. Most child therapists, as they begin to form an attachment to the child, have rescue fantasies something like "If only I could take this child home with me, I could save him/her from the psychological pits." The unspoken part of this fantasy is, "The parents did such a bad job of raising the child, I certainly could do better." As the therapist becomes fond of the child he/she might become angry at the parents for "causing" such past and current pain in the child.

Just as the parents might become jealous of the therapist, so might the therapist become jealous of the parents, who have so much time with the child. In the face of these feelings toward the parents, the therapist might want to adopt an isolationist position; "Just leave us alone in our therapy room where we can do our private thing. We can work out the problem alone. Let the rest of the world, particularly the parents, go by." Such an attitude would certainly disrupt communication with the parents.

Finally, the desirability of preserving confidentiality of both the child's revelations to the therapist and the parents' revelations to either therapist or a separate therapist works against open communication.

So what do you do? Foremost, the parents must be kept an active part of the treatment for both theoretical and practical reasons so, in spite of all the barriers enumerated above, the clinic staff must make every effort to establish and maintain a good working relationship with the parents. The theoretical reason why parents must be included in treatment is discussed above, namely, the child does not live in isolation and therefore cannot be most efficiently treated in isolation. The practical reason is that the parents are the legal guardians of the child (except in rare cases where that right is removed by the court), and *they* decide if and when the child receives treatment. If they do not consent to treatment, all of our good, professional, and reasonable ideas are so much wind.

Even if the parents are seen by a mental health worker other than the child's therapist, the therapist should work closely with the parents from the very beginning of treatment or, if possible, from evaluation. The therapist should have sessions with the parents to explore their perception of the problem, their ideas about possible solutions, and the therapist's ideas about problems and possible solutions. The outcome of these sessions is an agreement as to what will be tried and what each party's role in the treatment will be. It is often helpful if the therapist and parents together set a fairly short time, 4 to 6 weeks of treatment, after which time all will take another look at the problem and how the intervention is going. This helps parents in the beginning to avoid an often serious barrier to making a commitment to treatment, namely, the feeling that they are committing themselves to an endless and prohibitively expensive enterprise. It is especially important to involve the traditional father in this decision-making process, since he is often more removed psychologically from the problem but very involved financially if he is the one who makes the family's financial decisions.

The therapist needs to be aware of all the potential feelings he/she may have toward the parents and the parents toward him/her, not that the therapist reveals to the parents or expects the parents to reveal to him/her each little feeling, as such a practice would be burdensome, impractical, unproductive, and endless. Rather, the therapist needs to know the possibilities so as to be aware of when any of these feelings on his/her part or the parents' part becomes a serious barrier to communication in the therapeutic effort. In that case the therapist and/or the mental health worker seeing the parents could deal directly with the attitude or feeling.

As a side note, the beginning therapist should become aware of the potentially valuable therapeutic use of his/her own feelings toward the parents. It is possible that the therapist's emotional reactions to the parents are in some ways parallel to the child's reactions to them. The therapist can use the feelings to understand better what the child is experiencing in the parent-child relationship. From that understanding could evolve some work with the child around learning more adaptive ways of dealing with his/her emotional reactions to the parents and of interacting with them.

I usually follow a procedure that is useful in promoting close cooperation without threatening confidentiality too greatly. I try to conduct all feedback and planning meetings with everyone present—i.e., child's therapist, parents, child, and if involved, the parents' mental health worker. This creates some problems in that the meeting is sometimes cumbersome and the participants may not feel comfortable saying what is on their minds with everyone present. However, the practice has advantages. Each participant knows what is said to whom and does not have to speculate about what might be said at a meeting at which he/she was not present. In addition, the message is clear from the format that everyone has a share in the problem and its solution.

WHAT ARE SOME POTENTIAL PROBLEMS BETWEEN THE CHILD'S THERAPIST AND THE CHILD'S PARENTS?

By being aware of potential problems in relating to parents, the therapist perhaps can prevent some difficult situations from developing. Some parents have a great need to talk with someone about their personal concerns. If the parent also has high need for nurture and is jealous of the child's relationship with the therapist, he/she may attempt to get some of the therapist's time and attention. A frequent parent maneuver is to ask to see you for a few minutes at the beginning of the child's session. Those few minutes, even with the child present, can often stretch into a significant amount of the child's time. The parent may use the child's problems as an entree but then swing into his/her own issues. You can become frustrated because you want to get on with your child session, the parent feels pressure to keep you engaged in listening to him/her, and the child grows angry at being pushed off the stage. One tactic to avoid getting into this situation is to offer the parent a few minutes at the end of the child's session if the parent approaches you at the beginning. This would give you the opportunity to speculate with the child about what is on the parent's mind. If the parent attempted to prolong the contact at the end of the child's session, then at least the child's time is not being taken away. You will also be able to use other commitments as a reality factor in terminating the time with the parent. If the parent persists in taking your time, some decisions need to be made. Primarily, you need to understand why the parent is behaving this way. Are the issues the parent brings up parent-child related and do you need to set up some conferences with the parent? Is the parent deliberately or unconsciously wanting to hurt the child by stealing time and attention from him/her? Does the parent need and/or want therapy for him/herself? If you can answer these questions, you will have a better chance of helping the parent and the child.

If the parent needs and desires therapy for him/herself, you might be tempted to become the parent's therapist, particularly if you are in private practice instead of on a clinic team. Being both the parent's and the child's therapist has some advantages in that you can gain a more complete understanding of what goes on in the family and you can coordinate the child's and parent's treatment goals as well as the means of achieving these goals. There are, however, some danger spots. Preserving confidentiality with material from both parent and child may be difficult if for no other reason than just keeping track of what you heard from whom. Parents and children inevitably have conflict. As your emotional envolement with both parent and child can never be exactly equal, you will tend to side more with one than the other, to the detriment of your working relationship with the other. If these conflicts come to court, such as in a custody hearing, and you have to get on the stand, you are in a no-win position. You might save yourself some personal stress and avoid potential damage to your clients if you make arrangements for another therapist to work with the parent.

Child custody battles can sometimes put the therapist in a difficult position. Each parent attempts to enlist the therapist on his/her side, to convince the therapist that he/she is correct and that the other parent is the evil one. If the child has complained bitterly about one parent, the therapist may be tempted to advocate for the child in the courtroom. Obviously, if the therapist testifies against the parent who is bringing the child to therapy, the therapy is likely to terminate. The therapist may not have any choice if the parent gives permission and the therapist receives a subpoena to testify in court. It might be helpful if the therapist realizes that unless he/she has been part of a complete custody evaluation, he/she does not have the full picture. Information about the parents obtained primarily through the child can be quite skewed; certainly information from only one parent will be. In general, I favor an open approach to the problem, that is, to tell the parent, with the child present, what I think about the information I have but point out that I have only a very limited view. Of course, openness does not go so far as to violate the child's confidence. If, for example, the child had told you but not the custodial parent that he/she did not want to stay with that parent and you told the parent, you would not only violate the child's confidence but would almost certainly bring about abrupt termination of therapy. Dealing with parents in the midst of a custody dispute requires utmost delicacy. Once you give testimony in court, you simply have to reassess the new situation to see if you can play any useful role in the child's treatment. Because of all these difficulties, many child therapists try to avoid court involvement in custody disputes unless they are specifically engaged in custody evaluations.

What if in your sessions with the parents they tell you what you want to hear about how they deal with their child around rules, discipline, and positive interactions, but then you gather from the child or other sources that family matters are not as presented by the parents? To compound the situation, suppose that you believe that the parents are interacting with the child in ways you feel are clearly detrimental to the child (but not to the extent of child abuse)? You might be trying, for example, to help build the child's self-confidence, and you discover that the parents are directly or indirectly telling the child that he/she is a worthless, rotten kid. Certainly, you would feel angry with the parents and frustrated that you could not control the child's environment. What can you do? Confronting the parent directly is probably what you would feel like doing, but this would likely accomplish only one thing: termination of therapy. Except in the few instances where child therapy is court-ordered, the parents control whether their child continues in therapy or not, so maintaining a working relationship with the parents is essential. Berating them is not a way to maintain a good relationship. The first move I would recommend in this situation is to set up some family therapy sessions. When your goal is to change interaction patterns between parents and child, successful family therapy is a good way to accomplish the goal. In family sessions the tone of parent-child interactions is likely to emerge, and all will begin seeing how the parents ignore or put down the child. You will probably also see what the child does to elicit and perpetuate this behavior from the parents and what role the siblings play in the interaction patterns.

In my experience it is often difficult to involve in family therapy the kinds of families described above. Reasons for resistance to family therapy could be feelings of threat from outsiders who will find fault with their parenting, anger at the child, just not caring enough to put the energy into family sessions, involvement of a parent in his/her own problems (e.g., alcoholism), or any combination of these reasons. So, failing to engage the family in family therapy, you can only continue your efforts to present clearly to the parents your view of their child's problem and what he/she needs. You will probably make better progress by applauding and expanding on what positive things the parents tell you they do with their child than by challenging them. That is, if you believe they are not giving enough attention to the child but they say they are, you could say something like, "It's great that you are giving Billy that time because that is exactly what he needs. In fact, he could be helped with even more of that kind of help from you." You might then explore other ways the parents could give time and attention to the child. Still, you will probably find that it is an uphill struggle, that it is extremely difficult for the child therapist to change parent behavior without direct intervention such as through family therapy. One of the things most difficult for the beginning child psychotherapist to learn is to live with the frustration of not being able to effect changes in major areas of the child's life. Not that one gives up trying, but sometimes one can get professional satisfaction only from the limited amount of help one is able to give the child in sessions with him/her.

Many children in psychotherapy have divorced parents. Perhaps they are both interested in being involved in the child's therapy yet are not communicating with each other. They may attempt to engage you as a liaison or messenger between them. It is often tempting to go along with this role because it is in the child's interest that the parents do indeed communicate about the child, particularly, from your point of view, around psychotherapy issues. To fall into the liaison role, however, ultimately abets the parents in avoiding talking to each other when they really need to work through this communication problem themselves.

What Can You Say to a Parent about the Child and Still Preserve the Child's Confidentiality?

The therapist really must, I am convinced, have sessions with the parents, even if the parents have their own mental health worker at the clinic. The parents want to learn of the child's progress as seen by the therapist, and the therapist wants to learn of the child's progress as seen by the parents at home, in school, and in the neighborhood. Usually the child will be concerned with privacy at a different level from that of the parents. The child may, for example, not want the parent to hear about some secret he/she has told the therapist, such as a misdeed, some violation of a family rule, anger at one of the parents, a fight with a sibling, or a secret wish; whereas the parent is more interested in global assessment of the child's progress, such as controlling impulses, becoming more independent, becoming less fearful, or growing in self-confidence.

If you believe that your meeting with the parents must take place, then you should not ask the child for permission to talk with his/her parents lest the child say no. Here is a suggestion as to how the session with the child prior to the therapist-parent meeting might go. You say, "Your parents want to know how you are getting along in the sessions here. When I meet with them, I will not tell them any of your secrets or specifically what we do, but I plan to tell them in general terms how I think you are getting along. I'll tell them we play and talk and have gotten to know each other pretty well. I plan to say to them, '[child's name] seems to be growing up well and getting better control over his anger. He still has a bit of trouble and will continue working on it. I think he gets down on himself too much, which is too bad, because I think he has many reasons to feel really good about himself.' Is it OK if I say something like that?" If the child says no, then say, "Well, I have to tell them *something*. What do you want me to say?" If the child says OK to what you plan to say, ask if there is anything else he/she would like you to add.

At this point you might invite the child to sit in on the session and hear for him/herself what is said. In my experience many children do not want to sit in on the parent conference. Perhaps the offer is enough to reassure them of your intention to preserve their privacy, or perhaps they know they will be too uncomfortable sitting and listening to significant people talk about them. If the child does sit in on your session with the parent, then you and the child might have a profitable rehash of the meeting during your next therapy session. Discussion could be about the content of what you and the parents said, about the emotional tone of the meeting, and about the child's feelings during the meeting.

At the start of the parent-therapist meeting, you would explain that in order to preserve the child's confidentiality you will not be giving any private details from the therapy sessions but that the child has agreed to some general statements about your view of his/her progress. I have never worked with parents who did not accept this structure.

What Can You Do with Information about the Child that You Receive Directly, or through a Third Party, from the Parents?

If in a spirit of openness, you tell the child at once what you have heard, then you will avoid the trap of waiting, waiting for the child to bring up the material, while the child is perhaps waiting, waiting for you to bring it up. Once the material is on the table between you, then you and the child may or may not decide to deal further with it at that time.

How Do You Deal with Requests from Parents to Watch or View Tapes of a Session with the Child?

The issues here are complex because of a conflict of rights. The parents have a right to know what is going on with their child; the child is theirs, after all, and they are legally responsible for the child's health and welfare. The child, on the other hand, has a right to privacy, particularly in therapy sessions where he/she may be talking about or playing out family scenes that he/she does not want the parents to know about. One solution is to obtain the child's permission to have the parents watch. However, the child's play could be significantly altered by such knowledge and, more important, it would disturb the special and private, my-time, my-therapist context of the therapy relationship.

I have tried several approaches to this problem and have found that it works best not to allow the parent to watch—ever. It might make it easier on the therapist to invoke a rule: "Parents do not watch their children's therapy sessions in this clinic." If the parents have difficulty accepting this rule, it could provide an entree into understanding the parent-child relationship, the parents' feelings about the child, the clinic, and the child's therapist, and the parents' trust in the whole process. With this stance about observation, the clinician must be willing to accept the possibility that the parent will not live with this rule and will withdraw the child from treatment.

WHAT ARE SOME BENEFITS AND POTENTIAL PROBLEMS IN MAKING HOME VISITS?

Benefits

1. The therapist sees the child in his/her natural setting; the therapist learns how the child interacts with family members at home.
2. The child takes pride in showing the therapist "my toys, my bed, my pet, my family."
3. Many contextual cues and meanings are acquired by the therapist. That is, after the home visit, when the child talks in therapy session about the events at home, the therapist can visualize and obtain a better feel for what happened.
4. The therapist gets to meet the child's siblings.
5. The child is proud to show off his/her therapist. It makes the child feel special to receive a visit from an important adult in his/her life.

Potential Problems

1. The setting is not really natural with the therapist present. The child and the family might put on their "best behavior."
2. The therapist is likely to be treated as a guest in the home, since the parents know the role of host best and may feel uncomfortable or unable to allow the therapist to be a silent observer.

3. The child may not like to share his/her therapist with others.
4. If the home is of a different SES (socio-economic status) or if the family is of a different racial or ethnic group than the therapist, the therapist may react with nonverbal communication to elements in the house and home life that are different or new to the therapist. These may be negative reactions, or the family might perceive them to be negative reactions, which would then put strains on the therapist-family relationship.

WHAT CONTACT DO YOU HAVE WITH RELATIVES OTHER THAN THE PARENTS?

Clearly if the child's grandparents(s), aunt, uncle, or other relative is the child's primary caretaker, then everything written about parents in this section will apply to them. Otherwise, the answer to the question depends on the immediacy of the relative in the child's life. Grandparents who live across the country and who visit the child's family once a year would probably not be involved in the child's psychotherapy. In fact, their involvement might unnecessarily complicate matters, especially if the child's parents and grandparents have major unresolved issues between them. The child's problem, for example, might be used by a grandparent to put the blame on their child or child-in-law for the problem. The child's parents certainly do not need that. The less the grandparents know about the details of the child's treatment the better. These same comments about cross-country grandparents would apply to other cross-country relatives such as aunts, uncles, and emancipated siblings.

If, on the other hand, the grandparents live in the same house with the child, then they will probably need to become involved in the child's treatment. Certainly, if family therapy were the mode of treatment, they will be included in the family sessions along with siblings and anyone else living under the same roof. If the child is being seen in individual psychotherapy sessions, the therapist might consider occasionally including other household adult relatives in interpretive sessions so they can understand and facilitate the treatment goals. Some therapists also include siblings in such sessions. If all of the household members, including the child client, are included in sessions with the child's therapist, then the therapist should be well armed with family therapy skills, since he/she will have to deal with family dynamics. The line between family feedback sessions and family therapy becomes blurred. Probably the reason the child therapist in the traditional child guidance clinic of the 1940s through 1960s did not meet with the entire family, and sometimes not even with the parents, is that most child therapists of that era did not have family therapy training and skills.

Relatives who live somewhere between cross-country and under the same roof can be included in the treatment process in proportion to how involved and influential they are in the child's life. Relatives can be a good source of information about a child and his/her family. A grandparent or an aunt who lives in the same town, for example, might have new knowledge and a different perspective on the child's life from those in the immediate household. The process of obtaining this information from a relative is sometimes complicated. First, the parents would have to know about and approve of the interview between clinician and relative; next, the interview needs to be arranged and held; then the parents will want to know what the relative said; finally, the child needs to be informed of all this. Quite possibly the relative will want feedback from the clinician about what the clinician thinks is wrong with the child and what is being done in therapy, but the clinician cannot ethically give that information without consent from the parent and, optimally, also from the child. If the relative's involvement continues into the treatment phase, the clinician must carry on the same juggling act. It is no wonder that most child clinicians do not generally make good use of relatives in the treatment process.

Chapter 8

SCHOOL

WHAT ARE THE DANGERS AND ADVANTAGES OF
CONTACT BETWEEN THE CHILD'S THERAPIST AND PEOPLE AT THE
CHILD'S SCHOOL?

A child's life is divided between home and school. In fact, from Monday through Friday the number of hours a child spends at school equals or exceeds the waking hours spent at home. Since the environment and expectations are often quite different in school, at home, and in the therapy room, the child's behavior may be quite different in these settings. The therapist may well need and want to get information from school and share information with school personnel, just as the therapist wants and needs to understand the child's behavior within the family. There are, however, some potential dangers in establishing a connection between the mental health system in which the child is being treated and the school system in which the child is being educated.

When the school personnel learn that the child is in psychotherapy, it is possible that the child will acquire a negative label: "mentally ill," "emotionally disturbed," "crazy," or worse. A possible negative consequence of such a label is the school personnel's expectation of "sick" behavior. They may expect manifestations of deviant behavior or problems with conformity or limited achievement. They may begin either to coddle or to fear the child or treat him/her in an unsual or "special" way, in order to keep the child stabilized or to avoid confronting emotional situations. The child in turn may just live up (or down) to these expectations of deviancy. Labeling the child may also lead to the school personnel's labeling of parents as "bad," "crazy," or "inadequate." Such labeling might then result in the school staff reacting differently toward the parents and even possibly toward other siblings in the family.

Another potential problem of therapist-school contact might be a child's confusion about two aspects of his/her life that are difficult to integrate. Sometimes child clients totally ignore the therapist during a school visit, not because they are embarrassed but because they simply do not know how to behave toward the therapist in the school setting.

An additional potential danger is that the child may feel intruded on. "So many people know about my problem, are watching me, talking about and judging me. I wish they'd just get off may case and leave me alone—let me be like the other kids." All of this attention could cause the child to inflate a problem out of proportion to other aspects of his/her life that are going well.

The child also may question confidentiality of information the therapist and teacher have about him/her. For example, the child may wonder, "What will my therapist say about me to the teacher? Will the teacher know when I complain about school or that I wet my bed? What will the teacher say about me? Will she tell my therapist that I tore up my test or got in a fight at recess?"

Despite potential dangers, I believe the advantages of therapist-school contact generally outweigh the disadvantages. Contact through a school visit gives the therapist a valuable opportunity to learn about an important aspect of the child's life. The therapist will learn firsthand how the school people view the child. Specifically, the therapist can learn about the child's interpersonal relationships with peers and with authority figures, about the child's academic achievement, and about the child's coping styles.

Contact with the child's educational system serves to remind the therapist that the child functions in a total but varied world—that strengths and difficulties may be discovered in various settings. In a word, the child is viewed as a total person rather than fragments of symptoms or as exclusively in the child-client role. The contact between therapist and school also gives the message to the child and the child's family that the therapist does not view the child in isolation in the therapy room.

Teachers and other school staff might feel some sense of relief that someone with special skills is working with the child about whom they have been concerned—that they do not have the entire responsibility for the child's psychological welfare. They may also appreciate having a consultant to call on for help. If the child is misbehaving at school, e.g., fighting or stealing, the school people may hope that the therapist will change this unacceptable behavior. (It would be wise for the therapist not to encourage such expectations, however, unless changing the child's behavior at school is a primary goal of the psychotherapy.)

An additional advantage of therapist-school contact is that the teacher and others at school may learn of some psychological factor such as a deep and persistent feeling (e.g., anger, loneliness, negative feeling about self), some unmet need, or an internal or external conflict that makes the child's behavior more understandable, more acceptable, and possibly more manageable.

Finally, spending time in a school will help the beginning therapist keep a perspective on normal child behavior and development. The therapist can see other children the same age as the client to learn how they cope with school demands, how they develop physically, how they interact with peers, how they control their impulses, and so on. The therapist might discover, for example, that there are many 8-year-old boys who draw pictures of spaceships with laser guns destroying other ships and that this may not necessarily represent significant anger or pathological aggression when seen in his/her client.

How Can You Be Effective in Working with the Personnel at the Child's School?

A systems view is helpful for the child psychotherapist who is interacting with the people at the client's school. The therapist who views the school as an entity with specialized parts (roles) for completing tasks and maintaining morale, with formal and informal channels of communication, and with a characteristic style of interacting with other agencies will be in a better position to judge the possibilities for effecting change in the child's school and to prevent potentially destructive relationships from developing.

The educational system and the mental health system have different goals, which could cause conflict between teacher and therapist. For example, a primary goal of the school system is to educate all of the children. A primary goal of the mental health system is to help individuals solve emotional and interpersonal problems. These goals do not necessarily conflict and may, in fact, be parallel. Nevertheless the child psychotherapist who forgets the primary goal of the school system will be facing frustration at not having everyone in the school system focused primarily on helping the child client resolve intra- and interpersonal problems.

A common example of systems conflict arises when the beginning child therapist encounters difficulty in trying to schedule therapy sessions during school hours. With the primary goal in the therapist's mind of helping the child resolve emotional problems, the new therapist might become upset at the teacher's reluctance to have the child miss an hour or two of academic instruction every week. Since the primary goal of the education system is to educate the child, the teacher might justifiably feel that missing so much school is counterproductive. Actually most children who come to mental health centers have low self-esteem that is often made worse by academic failure, so scheduling psychotherapy appointments during school hours may indeed be contrary to mental health goals as well as to educational goals. The therapist can help resolve this situation by being aware of the conflicting goals of the mental health system and the school system and setting up a joint meeting with teacher and parents to work out a time for clinic visits that does not subvert either the educational or the mental health goals.

Although personnel in both the mental health system and the school system are highly invested in promoting growth in children, communication between thereapist and teachers can be difficult for several reasons. Each profession has its special vocabulary. Generally, those outside a profession are confused and even "turned off" by that profession's jargon. If child therapists use some of the education vocabulary, it might facilitate acceptance by school people. At the very least the therapist could avoid erecting barriers by not using mental health jargon with educators either orally or in psychological reports. Since most professionals use their special vocabulary automatically, it may facilitate a working relationship if the therapist acknowledges this with the other professional and asks for help in avoiding the use of jargon.

Communication may be distorted by issues involving expertise and/or power. I suggest that the best way to work well with teachers is to recognize them as fellow professionals. Teachers generally know a great deal about child behavior and development and certainly know far more than the usual child psychotherapist about how children learn and fail to learn academic material. With a respect for the teacher's general professional knowledge and special knowledge of the therapist's client, the therapist can establish a professional colleague relationship that will greatly facilitate exchange of information about the child. You can do a better job of understanding and helping your child client with information from the child's teacher, and the teacher can likewise do a more effective educational job with information and understanding from you.

Communication can be improved by the therapist's awareness of the teacher's experience and frame of reference. I would recommend that every child therapist, early in his/her training, spend *at least* one full school day with a teacher. The benefits of this experience are that the therapist will realize how little he/she knows about educating children, the therapist will recapture some of what the child experiences sitting in school all day, and finally, the teacher will appreciate the therapist for trying to learn all of the above.

There are other potential barriers to a professional working relationship between teacher and therapist. The therapist who is sensitive to these potential issues may be able to avoid some of the problems that can interfere with good professional collaboration. Some of the same preconceptions and jealousies that can interfere with the therapist-parent relationship can interfere with the therapist-teacher relationship.

The teacher may envy the therapist's luxury of working one-to-one with the child. "If I could devote my time exclusively to Billy, I could do great things with him too. But what am I supposed to do with the other 31 children in my class?" The teacher may think, "If that therapist is doing such a great job, how come Beth is not improving in her behavior? What good is therapy anyhow?" Some teachers may be defensive because of a fear that the therapist will blame them for causing, or at least perpetuating, the child's problem. The therapist, on the other hand, may be jealous of the teacher's extended contact. "If I worked with Mike five hours a day, five days a week, I could do wonders."

Unless the therapist has had classroom teaching experience, or at least has been married to a teacher, he/she rarely appreciates (emotionally, not just intellectually) the fact that the teacher cannot be a full-time child therapist and that he/she has responsibility for 31 other children. Also, while the effective teacher is sensitive to each child's emotional needs, he/she is primarily responsible for facilitating an increase of academic skills and knowledge in all of the children in his/her classroom, not just in one child. The teacher cannot give one child the kind of special attention, instruction, and emotional support that the therapist might wish, and it is unrealistic for the therapist to expect it.

The therapist can be alert to one other potential situation that often interferes with good teacher-therapist communication. If the child in therapy has the kind of problem that interferes with the learning process or disrupts the classroom procedure, the good teacher already has tried every professional skill available to help the child. Often the teacher has had consultation from fellow professionals. Nothing works. In desperation the teacher refers the child for outside mental health assistance. The feeling often is "I've tried everything possible and can't make any progress. Let someone else take the responsibility." Some weeks later the child gets connected with a mental health system.

Several scenarios can develop at this point. You, as the child's new therapist, may come into the school full of ideas about what the teacher can do to improve the child's emotional adjustment. Resistance, even resentment, on the part of the teacher would be most understandable. Or the teacher may view you as the expert who will provide the "magical" answers, and he/she will attempt to get you to suggest immediate and specific solutions. While appealing to both the therapist's ego and his/her intentions, such a response is ultimately detrimental. Magical solutions seldom work, and the collegial role between therapist and teacher is undermined. At other times the teacher may view the conference as a cathartic opportunity, overwhelming the new therapist with everything that has been tried, the terribleness of the child, and the impossibility of any change. Such emotional release may be necessary for the frustrated teacher and will provide the therapist with specific information about the child's behavior and the response such behavior may elicit from others. However, little will be gained if the exchange between teacher and therapist does not move beyond this point. You are the child's therapist, not the teacher's therapist, and the focus needs to shift back to the child.

Ideally, the first contact with the teacher would be a flow of informaton about the child from the teacher to you during which you appreciate what the teacher has experienced with the child, and then you both try to understand the child together. As the teacher slowly becomes engaged in puzzling out this child, he/she may come up with some new suggestions and be more ready to hear suggestions from you. The ideal relationship between you and the teacher is that of ongoing collaboration between professional equals in a common effort of helping the child client.

What Can You Tell the Child about Your School Contact?

I suggest that you be as open with the child as possible. Tell the child why you are going to call or visit the school, what you want to know from the teacher, and what you plan to say. Get the child's okay. If the child balks at the idea of your visit, find out why and alter what you will say at school to reduce his/her anxiety. If the child does not truly have final veto over your visit, he/she needs to know why it is in his/her interests that you are contacting the school. Perhaps you could discuss the child's preference regarding the time of the visit, i.e., before or after school when the child is not there or during class when you could meet his/her teacher and the child could share his/her work with you. In any case, the important goal is to keep the child's trust in your special relationship. Disagreement about this issue would become, like any issue, grist for your therapeutic work with the child.

If you are planning to visit the child's classroom during school hours, it is really helpful to ask the child how you should behave toward him/her when you are there. Does the child want you to ignore him/her? Does the child want to introduce you to the class? If you are introduced, what label does the child want to use for your relationship: friend, therapist, . . ? At least one child in an elementary class can be counted on to ask, "Is that your Mom/Dad?" What should you say if the other children ask you who you are? You could avoid some awkward moments and possible embarrassment to the child if you and the child have worked out your answers and his/her answers to these questions before the visit. It might be helpful if the child identified for you the most important kids to him/her in the room. These could be both friends and enemies. You could then observe their interactions and also know to whom the child was referring in later therapy sessions.

If your relationship with the child is based on openness, then of course you would give feedback to the child after your school visit. It would be helpful to hear how the child experienced your visit, how teachers and peers might have acted differently toward the child during or after the visit, and whether the child wished for something to be different about the visit. On the other side, the child would want to know how you view the school, the teachers and staff, the physical setting, and the other children. Anticipate what you will choose to tell the child about your objective and subjective observations. In general, the school visit by the child's psychotherapist can open up a whole new area of common experience with the child and therefore lead to a better understanding of him/her.

Do You Need the Parents' Permission before Contacting the School?

Almost certainly, yes. Many schools, in fact, can not speak about their pupils with people from outside agencies without written parental permission in their files. For both legal and ethical reasons your clinic must also have written consent to pass along any information to another person or agency. As with the child, complete openness with parents as to what you hope to accomplish by a school contact and what material you plan to pass along to the school personnel is suggested. After the contact you might enhance your working relationship with the parents by sharing with them the results of your visit.

Whom Do You Contact at the School?

If you view the school from a systems perspective, then you would learn whom to contact in order to plug into the system most effectively. Schools these days generally have personnel who deal with special problems of their pupils: counselors, nurses, psychologists, social workers. You might make the first contact with the person in your own profession. If there is no such person on the school staff, the principal or assistant principal would know whom to call in order to set up a visit. One temptation therapists have is to call the child's teacher directly. This seems like a logical move but is often a bad idea. Most schools, in order to keep the wheels turning in some orderly manner, have procedures for dealing with outside agencies. The therapist who deliberately or innocently circumvents these procedures is off to a bad start in future dealings with the school personnel. Once you are in contact and have learned the protocol and personalities at that particular school, you can be more effective in exchanging information.

WHAT DO YOU ACTUALLY DO AT THE SCHOOL?

The answer depends, of course, on what you wish to accomplish in your contact with the school. If you wish to learn about the child's academic functioning, peer relationships, and classroom atmosphere and to exchange information with school personnel, then you might set up a visit that includes observing the child in the classroom and at recess (or other free time), with these activities adjacent to a time when the teacher(s) and other personnel directly involved with the child are free to talk with you. Sometimes a school counselor, social worker, or other designated staff person can set up a special meeting for you to exchange information with everyone who deals with the child at the school. It may be useful to include the child's parents at such a meeting. If such a formal staffing is set up, it would be helpful to have made a more informal prior visit just to have a feel for the school and the child's teachers and peers and some familiarity with the physical setup. Because of busy and conflicting schedules, it usually requires a great deal of effort to set up a formal meeting between all the concerned parties. Before trying to arrange such a meeting the therapist might ask, Is a meeting the best way to exchange information and do the benefits of having everyone meet together outweigh the inconvenience inherent in setting up the meeting?

The teacher has a wealth of information about your client because of his/her regular contact with the child and the informal norms in his/her head about age-expected behavior and adjustment. You will further your personal relationship with the teacher by acknowledging this fund of information. To obtain information about the child, whether in a formal staffing or in an informal conference with the teacher, you might have some specific, open-ended questions in mind, such as How is the child's academic work? How does he/she organize work, focus on it, and follow through on projects? Is his/her impulse control at expected age level? How does the child relate to authority? How does the child get along with peers? Don't forget to ask about the child's strengths and areas of success and what the teacher likes about the child.

Once the first formal visit is made, you probably can keep in direct phone contact with the child's main teacher or others who have continuous interaction with the child. Having continuous contact will enable you to maintain up-to-date information and understand the child as he/she functions in the real world.

How Do You Keep from Getting Caught between School and Parents?

Probably the best way to learn to recognize and handle the situation where you are in the middle of a power struggle between parents and school is to get caught there once. The second time this begins to develop you will be gun-shy. If you view the situation as a conflict between two systems, family and educational, then it might help you to be a bit more objective, that is, not get caught up on a personal level. As an outsider, from a third system, you can be certain that taking sides will most often be disastrous because it results in either the school or the family becoming the "odd-man-out."

Both the parents and the school people know that you have the child's best interests at heart and will make an appeal to you on the ground that the other system is doing something detrimental to the child. If you see this developing, you can take a neutral stand, which is easier said than done. Perhaps you could turn the best-interest-of-the-child argument around to convince both the school people and the parents that it would be in the best interest of the child if they solved this between them. If you feel really brave (and skilled) you might volunteer to mediate a session between the two systems. Otherwise, you might back off on the grounds that the mental health system you are in is not in a position to side with the family or the school in their dispute. Such a stand might divert some of the heat from you to the agency where you are working.

What Do You Do if You Judge the Teacher to Be Harmful to the Child?

In spite of all the above discussion about teamwork between professional colleagues, there will undoubtedly be some time during your career when you encounter what you consider a bad teacher—someone who is harmful to the child. (No doubt, too, there are situations where the teacher judges the psychotherapist to be harmful to the child, but I shall let someone from the education establishment write about that.) The situation of the "bad" teacher may have developed because of a mismatch between the child's personality or needs and the teacher's personality and teaching style. At other times the behavior of either the child or the teacher may evoke such strong negative reactions in the other that the resolution of these feelings may be almost impossible.

As the child's therapist, you have a responsibility to advocate for the child. It would be well to remember that you are not part of the school system and that you need to increase your familiarity with the particular school. Knowledge of both the school and of the individual teacher is vital. If you have formed a close working relationship with another person in the school, such as a social worker, nurse, psychologist, or another teacher, it would be helpful to consult with this trusted professional as to what is going on with the child's teacher and how you might best proceed with the problem. This is tricky because, for ethical reasons, you would not want to reveal specifics about your concerns, and you certainly do not want to inject rumor and turmoil into the school. Yet you need information and advice about what to do. The phrase "proceed with caution" comes to mind. Lacking a confidant in the school, you might consider the following steps.

First, be sure of your facts. If possible, gather some firsthand information, or at least information from more than one source. If you rely entirely on the child's report or the parent's complaints, you might be getting drawn into a position of taking sides in a family-school struggle.

Second, discuss your concerns with the teacher. This is a difficult step because the teacher, who is likely already aware of his/her uncomfortable relationship with the child, may justifiably feel attacked and become quite defensive. A conference with the teacher around his/her interaction with the child could have some negative consequences if the teacher then picks on the child or refuses to have further contact with the therapist. On the other hand, the conference may have the opposite effect, namely, that the teacher feels on the spot and is careful not to interact with the child in a destructive way. Change in the teacher-child interaction is most likely to occur if the difficulties have arisen because of a teacher's reaction to a child's unique behavior. Change is least likely to occur if the teacher's style of teaching and his/her personal philosophy of class management is at odds with your child client's individual needs.

Third, if discussion with the teacher has not resolved your concerns, then a conference with the school principal might be helpful for the child. One solution is for the child to be transferred to another teacher. If that is not possible, at least your concerns (with concrete information) will be on record with the school administration, so if there is a general pattern of behavior for this teacher, someone responsible in the system knows about it.

Fourth, you need to help the child cope with the teacher. It probably will not be helpful to encourage the child's rebellion since that sabotages adults' authority and rarely solves the problem. I have found it helpful to teach the child ways of indirectly coping with the teacher, such as fantasy, suppression, or keeping an eye to the future when the child will be out of the room that day and that year. It is helpful to point out to the child that he/she will *always* encounter some authority person in his/her life who is a "bad number," and in the child's best interest this person needs to be coped with indirectly and not taken on directly.

Chapter 9

POTENTIAL PROBLEMS

What Limits on the Child's Behavior Do You Set and how Can They Be Enforced?

The first task of the psychotherapist is to establish rapport with the client. Many beginning child psychotherapists are reluctant to set and firmly enforce limits on their client's behavior in the therapy room for fear that the child will not like them. An extreme example of this happened to a colleague in training with me. His 11-year-old client proceeded to attack a wall in the playroom with his hunting knife. The therapist simply watched during the hour as the child destroyed the wall with more and more frantic behavior. The child never returned to the clinic, and the speculation was that the boy became overwhelmed and thoroughly frightened by his own impulses. He needed help in controlling himself, not catharsis. In the long run and in the short run, it helps the child feel more secure when the therapist sets and enforces limits on behavior.

The therapist can make the job of rule enforcement easier if the therapy room is set up with minimum potential for destructive behavior. For example, if there are no darts with points, then a whole set of safety rules need not be established. Similarly, the therapist might wish to ask him/herself if it is necessary to have missile-shooting toys (guns), hard balls, exposed fluorescent lights, reachable microphones, and other hazards in the room. However, no room can be totally breakproof and no therapist hitproof, so the therapist must be prepared to set and enforce limits.

Usually it is best not to explain the rules limiting the child's behavior until the occasion arises. If the child threatens with words or, more often, with actions to hurt him/herself or the therapist or to break up the room or toys, then you might say something like, "You know, we don't have many rules in here, but there are three general rules: you can't hurt yourself, you can't hurt me, and you can't tear up the room."

In thinking about setting and enforcing limits the tendency is to think in terms of aggressive behavior. There are of course other behaviors that might require limitation by the therapist. Would you, for example, allow the child to disrobe, to urinate or defecate on the floor (which is certainly not without its aggressive features), run water on the floor, pour all the sand out the window, smear clay on the carpet or walls, masturbate, or take toys home from the therapy room? For any given child there might be a therapeutic reason not to limit one of these behaviors, but generally, it seems to me, the child would not be helped to adapt to our social world if he/she were allowed free rein of behaviors that flagrantly violate basic social convention.

Whatever limits the therapist sets, it is more effective if they are enforced firmly, consistently, and unemotionally. The therapist who gets into a personal power struggle with a child client ought to examine his/her reasons why this is happening and even explore the question of whether child psychotherapy is the proper business to be in. Winning a power struggle for the therapist's personal reasons has no place in child psychotherapy.

How Do You Deal with the Child's Aggressive Behavior?

Explaining the reason behind a limit may be helpful to the child. It should be easy for even the young child in therapy to understand that destroying the room and/or toys means that they will not be available for other children or for the same child next time. Not hurting self or others is a bit more difficult to explain on logical grounds that the child can understand. "It just isn't done" may be the level at which the therapist will have to leave it if the child asks why. In any case, beyond explaining the limit, the wise therapist is not pulled into an argument with the child.

The actual enforcing of the rules can be done in graduated steps: give the child a reminder of the rule, command the child to stop, physically restrain the child. The therapist holding the young child during a tantrum might repeat several times in a voice more calm than the therapist invariably feels, "I simply will not let you hurt yourself [me, the room]." It may be impossible to restrain physically an older child who is a good match for the therapist's strength and speed. The absolute last means the therapist has of enforcing a rule is exclusion from the therapy room, the clinic, and treatment. In 20 years of child therapy I have not had to go to that extreme.

In order to help the beginning therapist think about possible responses he/she might make in an actual therapy situation, the following cases are given. What would you do and say in each of these instances?

Episode 1

Frank, 4½ years old, has problems Erikson would describe as a struggle of wills: his will against others and his will against his own impulses. In this twenty-fifth session he is painting at the easel when he stops and with a mischievous grin says to the therapist, "You know, I could take this brush and paint and throw it all over you and the ceiling."

THERAPIST:

Episode 2

Debbie, 8 years old, an only child, is defiant and verbally abusive to parents, teachers, and other adults. She bullies smaller children. Near the end of the fifth session:

DEBBIE: "I'm going to take this doll home [small 4″ mother doll]."
THERAPIST: "I know you would like to take the doll home, but there is a rule here that toys can't be taken out of the play room."
DEBBIE: "I don't care, I'm going to take it!" (She grips it tightly in hand and heads for the door.)
THERAPIST:

Episode 3

Bill, a large, husky 11-year-old, was referred for school failure and fighting with peers. Weekly therapy sessions have taken place over the past 10 weeks. The rules "you can't hurt yourself, you can't hurt me, and you can't tear up the room" had been explained early in the first session, because his rambunctious behavior in the first session threatened to violate the latter two rules. Nevertheless, he proceeded *each* session to break the limit once, usually by slugging the therapist in the arm or stomping on his foot. At session 11, Bill strides into the play room and swings the heavy punching bag, which hangs from the ceiling,into the head of the therapist. The therapist does and says the following:

THERAPIST:

For more extended and excellent writings on dealing with aggression I urge you to read the articles by Ray Bixler (1964), Haim Ginott (1964), and Allen (1942), chapter 7, "Problems Arising in Working With Aggressive Behavior," pp. 203–241.

What Should You Do about Physically Affectionate Behavior?

All models of child psychotherapy, I believe, would suggest that the therapist accept the child's affectionate behavior and the feeling behind it. Even when the child is using the affectionate approach not so much as an expression of genuinely felt affection but as a maneuver in some kind of power struggle with the therapist, the therapist would accept the overture at face value, recognize the ploy, and then help the child work out the control issue more overtly. Most therapists would not argue with the child by saying, "No, you don't like me, you are just saying that to get your own way," because the child, in addition to using the statement as a manipulation, may indeed like the therapist. A more productive response from the therapist might be, "Well, that's nice. I like you too." Then the therapist waits for the next move by the child. If it is a request from the child that is refused by the therapist, and the child says, "Why can't I? You don't really like me." The therapist can say, "Sure I do; that has nothing to do with your wanting to take that car home with you."

Assuming that the affectionate overture from the child is an expression of a genuine feeling of liking the therapist at that moment, the flip side of the feeling is wanting to be liked, to have the affection reciprocated. Child therapists of all theoretical persuasions would respond with some form of acceptance that conveys respect and caring for the child. Therapists would differ, however, on how active they would be in expressing direct affection. Personally, I could not remain the neutral, accepting, noncommittal therapist called for by Axline and Moustakas; I would actively reciprocate and express my affection for the child on the assumption that when the child expresses affection, he/she is also making an inquiry about my love toward him/her. This presents a good opportunity to communicate a feeling of positive regard for the child. (If the therapist does not, in fact, like the child, he/she has no business seeing that child in therapy.)

Probably most child therapists would agree that reciprocating negative emotions (e.g., anger, jealousy, and disgust) directly is not generally therapeutic. The argument might be made that just as one should not reciprocate negative emotions, one also should not reciprocate positive emotions; one should be consistent. I do not buy that argument because of the different nature of positive and negative emotions. The positive emotions of acceptance, regard, and love are central to the person's existential core; one must give and receive these emotions from early infancy to build basic trust in the world and to feel OK about oneself. It is often these very experiences of acceptance and love from others that the children in psychotherapy are lacking. In psychotherapy they receive some measure, preferably a full measure, of love and acceptance from the therapist. An emotion like anger, on the other hand, is less central to the person's being than is love. A person is angry at another because of what that other does or does not do to or for the person. The angry person does not generally reject the other as a person or else he/she would not bother getting angry with that person. For an excellent discussion of the degree of centrality of these emotions in the life space see Hanna Colm, "A Field-Theory Approach to Transference and Its Particular Application to Children," in Haworth (1964).

When the child makes affectionate overtures to the therapist, the therapist, after responding in appropriate kind, will be able to make better use of the exchange if he/she understands what underlies the overture. Is it manipulation? Is it display of affection to a transference object? Is it a spontaneous expression of a feeling? Is it a move seeking acceptance and affection from the therapist? Is it some combination of the above motives? The understanding of the child's motives will help the therapist know the child better and know what the therapist's *second* move should be.

The erotic components of affectionate feelings and behavior may present problems. Children communicate more easily and more often than do adults through physical means: touching, cuddling, hitting, spitting. Society spends enormous energy teaching the child to shift from physical to verbal means of communicating feeling. (Then the adult goes to a sensitivity group to learn how to touch again!) Probably the reason we socialize children to stop touching is because of our hang-up with sex. There are, however, some real problems. Holding a 6-year-old who crawls onto your lap in therapy is different from holding a 16-year-old of whatever sex on your lap. At what age does one draw the line? Just as a rule of thumb, when it begins tingling, be alert and disengage. Also, if the therapist notices the child getting sexually turned on, the therapist should cool it. There are two reasons for this move: (a) pedophilia is taboo and illegal and (b) the child (or adult) client should not have sexual needs met in the therapeutic relationship because therapy is a laboratory of life, not the real thing. Furthermore, a "mutual" erotic involvement between client and therapist, whatever the age, is inevitably not mutual. The therapist, through his/her power position, is usually taking advantage of the client to meet the therapist's needs, whether the involvement meets the client's needs or not.

One final note on physical means of expressing affection. Some children have already learned at an early age that touching is bad, and they feel that being touched intrudes on their privacy. The therapist must respect the child's discomfort with physical contact. If the therapist blasts through the child's comfort level in the belief that physical contact is natural and healthy, then he/she shows the child a lack of respect and acceptance, without which therapy cannot progress successfully.

WHAT CAN YOU DO WITH A BOSSY CHILD?

"No! Put that there." "Don't talk." "Give me that truck." "Raise your hand." "Make her drive the car here." Every child therapist sooner or later receives these commands. What do you do with the child, and what do you do with your own feelings?

To deal most effectively with the bossy child, the therapist needs to understand why the child is bossy. Is the child simply imitating a bossy person in his/her life? Is the child annoyed with the therapist's intrusiveness and trying to put a stop to it? Is the child attempting to counter feelings of inadequacy and impotence by controlling his/her environment, including the therapist? You can begin to test some of these hypotheses by going along with the child's directions to see how persistent the behavior is. If it goes on for some time, you might resist a bit, perhaps by ignoring the commands, to see how adamant or upset the child becomes. You might even try asking the child why he/she is giving orders. You could wonder out loud if he/she is bossed around a great deal. Even if you do not get the reason, you will get some idea about how aware the child is of his/her behavior or at least how willing the child is to admit the behavior.

After you have some idea about why the child is bossing you around, then how you respond will depend on your therapy goals. If you are trying to foster awareness in the child of his/her own behavior, you might simply comment on the fact that the child is giving a great number of orders. If you are attempting to foster awareness and acceptance of feelings in the child, you might make comments about how good it feels to be in control and boss people around (if that is indeed your understanding of what underlies the child's bossy behavior). If your goal is to help the child develop more adaptive social skills, you might comment on how most people do not like to be bossed around and that this behavior can lose the child some friends. You might drive this point home by becoming exaggeratedly bossy with the child yourself for just a few moments.

Since most people do not like to be bossed around, you will undoubtedly be annoyed with the child who does this to you. What you do with these feelings depends again on your therapy goals and techniques and also on the strength of these feelings. You might not say anything about your feelings if the goal is to help the child recognize his/her own feelings. If your goal is developing social skills, it would probably be helpful for the child to hear how bossy behavior makes people feel. If you do tell the child how you feel, it could be interpreted by the child as a hostile, critical remark. It is tricky to convince a child that you like him/her but you do not like his/her behavior. Nevertheless, you may be pushed beyond your tolerance level for being bossed. You may simply state that you are going to stop obeying the child's commands because you do not care to be ordered around. If you have a solid relationship with the child, it should survive that. At the very least this will let the child know you are human.

What Can You Do about the Child Who Wants to End the Session Early?

As with any single behavior, a child's leaving a therapy session early could have any one of a number of causes. So the therapist's first job is to understand why the child is leaving early, then base the response to that behavior on the underlying reason. The following are some possible reasons:

1. The child is angry at the therapist and thinks or says, "I'm mad at you and I'm not going to play with you any more."
2. The child doesn't want to clean up the room at the end of the session.
3. The child fears making the parent, who is transporting the child home, angry because of the long wait.
4. The child is bored.
5. The child has questions about his/her relationship with the therapist and wonders if the therapist will chase him/her, will insist on his/her staying, will become angry, will care enough to react at all.
6. The child is testing the limits, is curious as to the therapist's reaction to transgressions.
7. The child is starting to be afraid of becoming too close to or too dependent on the therapist.

8. The child is frightened about uncovering painful emotional material.
9. The child has to go to the bathroom.
10. The child is reacting to separation and wants control of it, "You can't leave me, I'm leaving you."
11. The child is looking forward to an exciting activity that follows the therapy hour (e.g., a party or a visit to the dentist).
12. The child is hungry or thirsty.
13. The child is getting sick.
14. The child wants to show the parent something.

When the child leaves early, the therapist might ask, as the child threatens to go or actually goes out the door, why he/she is leaving. The child may not be able or willing to say, but it seems the simplest way to start. I would follow the child in order to rule out external reasons like toilet needs or fear of keeping the transporting parent waiting. If the reason is not evident, I might say something like, "Well, I won't stop you from ending the hour, but I wish you wouldn't. I'll be in our room until our hour is over if you want to return; in any case I'll see you next time." If I am worried about a young or irresponsible child's safety, e.g., in wandering away from the clinic, I would keep a surreptitious eye on the child.

Then comes the tough part—trying to determine the cause(s) for the child's early departure. The therapist might approach the problem by reviewing the content of the hour, especially what was going on just prior to the child's leaving. Whatever the result of that effort at understanding the underlying causes, the reason will undoubtedly come up again, either it will be brought up by the therapist or, if it is important to the child, the child will continue trying to get that message through to the therapist.

What Do You Do when the Child Wants to Prolong the Time of the Session?

When a child delays leaving at the end of a session, either the child likes what is happening in the room with the therapist or there is something aversive outside following the session, or both. In my experience the reason has most often been the former. As with other behavior, the therapist needs to understand the child's motives in order to best help the child deal with the conflict between his/her desires and the realities of the world. Even without complete understanding of the child's motives, however, the therapist might say something like, "I know you don't want to go; I enjoy our time together too, but our time is up and I have to go. I'll see you next week." The therapist then puts the material away and heads for the door saying, "Come on." If the child still refuses to leave, the therapist just goes out the door and walks (slowly) to the waiting room to inform the parent of the situation. On occasions where the child goes home alone from the clinic, I have simply gone into a colleague's office and shut the door. (Then my colleague has to figure out a way to get me to leave.)

In general, I try to convey to the child in this situation an acceptance of the child's feelings about wishing to prolong the time and make an objective presentation of reality to the child through nonemotional actions that communicate a nonnegotiable position.

Why Do Children Steal Items from the Therapy Room and What Can You Do about It?

The behavior of taking something from the playroom can have very different meanings for different children. The lay person generally views stealing as a crime and one who steals as a criminal; therefore, children who steal are budding criminals and have a serious defect in their moral character. It is difficult for me to believe that a child who takes a toy from the therapy room is a young psychopath, although that is perhaps a possibility. The lifting of the toy is an expression of something else. Most often the reason has to do with the child's feeling about his/her relationship with the therapist. Possibly the child wants to test the limits in order to learn what the therapist is made of and how he/she will treat the child in an adversary situation. Perhaps the child is asking if the therapist really likes him/her enough to give the toy or enough to set and hold limits on the child. Perhaps the child is angry at the therapist and taking the toy is a hostile act. Maybe the child has impulse-control problems; he/she sees an attractive toy, wants it, and takes it. Are there other possible reasons? In any case, the child has probably used this behavior in the past in an attempt to gain whatever ends the child desires and therefore has a background of experiences with the reactions of elders and peers.

What do you do if the child takes or threatens to take something? First, I would suggest what *not* to do is get into a physical or emotional struggle with the child. Have you ever tried to take something forcibly out of the pocket of an active 7-year-old boy? You might succeed *if* the struggle is playful, *if* the child is not too determined, and *if* you are in good physical condition, but you may not want to risk the "ifs." So when the child asks to take some item from the therapy room or if you observe the child taking something, you might say, "I know you would like to have that, but we have a rule here because if everyone took something, pretty soon there would be nothing left to play with." I would advise the "natural consequences" approach of Rudolph Dreikurs (1964). If, after explaining the rule to the child and the rationale for the rule, the child persists, you would say in a matter-of-fact voice that if he/she takes the toy there will be no toys in the room for the next session. Then do not argue. If the child continues arguing, you can just pretend not to hear. If the child takes the toy anyway, I would suggest that you do not carry the struggle on, particularly in the waiting room where the parent would likely become involved in the issue. Next session you can have the child walk into an empty therapy room. I would not insist on the toy being brought back (that is just one of the material-consumption expenses in the child therapy business) but would state the reason for the empty room. For the next session you could return the toys. The cycle may be repeated as many times as necessary.

If the child takes something and the therapist discovers it later, he/she could say to the child at the opening of the next session something like "The father doll was missing last week and I'm worried that maybe you took it. I just need to let you know that if the toys keep disappearing, then we will have to remove *all* the toys." The child will probably deny having taken the doll. I would not argue with the child, but if I were quite certain that the child took the items, I would follow through with the toy removal plan. I have never had to resort to this extreme.

What Do You Do when the Child Brings Stolen Items into the Therapy Room?

There is no single best answer to this question because there are so many variables to consider before you react to the child who brings in a "hot" item. First, how do you *know* that the item is stolen? Does the child tell you it is? Do you have a strong *suspicion* that the item is stolen because of outside reports of the child's stealing or because the child has a pattern of bringing in items that he/she would be unlikely to own? Do you simply *wonder* whether the item belongs to your child client? Second, your reaction will vary depending on the value of the object. Is it an inexpensive pencil or an expensive watch? Third, did the child steal the item him/herself or did a friend steal it? A fourth variable to consider is how central stealing is to the child's clinical problem. Was stealing a primary complaint at intake or incidental to the presenting problem? Fifth, your response would vary with the communication style you had developed with the child. Are you communicating freely about almost everything? Do you usually introduce topics or wait for the child to take the initiative? Are you communicating directly with language or more symbolically through the play medium? Sixth, your reaction to the child will most certainly be influenced by your experience with and emotional reaction to theft. Have you ever been the victim of a theft? Do you believe stealing is a serious moral transgression or a passing stage for almost all kids—or both?

All of the above variables are peripheral to the actual therapeutic interaction you have going with the child. To know how to respond you have to know why the child is bringing the stolen item into therapy. Did he/she deliberately or inadvertently show you the object? Does the child want to see how you will react as a way of further defining your relationship? For example, the child might wonder if you will behave like a parent and scold him/her or make him/her return the item. Does the child feel guilty and want punishment from you? Is the child wanting to express anger in a way that will provoke you to respond? Is the child trying to show a "cool, macho" image? Is the child guiltless and simply wanting to show off a new possession?

Then too your response would depend on your relationship with the child. A few aspects of the relationship that would influence your response are how freely you communicate, how open you are with each other about discussing a wide range of topics, how safe the child feels with you, how angry the child is with you, and how dependent the child is on you.

Finally, you need to consider the goals of your therapy. If you are trying to increase your child's allocentrism, you might speculate with the child on the feelings of the victim or even have the child role-play the victim. If you are trying to increase the child's self-awareness, you might discuss what the child was thinking at each step of the theft. If the child stole the item as a hostile act toward the parents, you might help the child find more direct (and less self-destructive) ways to express his/her angry feelings. If it is an inexpensive item and the child had not brought in a stolen item before and it does not seem to be central to what is occurring in therapy, you might ignore it.

The variables and the possible ways you can respond are endless. Perhaps the best first response is to be as noncommittal as possible until you can ascertain a position on the major variables discussed here. Although the answer to the lead question is not given here, this section may help you consider the many facets of the issue. Finally, allow me to pass the buck: Ask your supervisor how he/she would suggest that you respond given all the variables involved.

How Can You Deal with the Child's Resistance to Therapy?

When the child in therapy stops playing, stops interacting with the therapist, and withdraws from the session either physically or psychologically, it may be labeled resistance. Temporary withdrawal may be for relatively minor reasons, but resistance is defined here as withdrawal in order to avoid the changes that occur in psychotherapy. All resistance is due to one underlying factor: the child perceives a threat to his/her self and becomes fearful of loss of self.

There are several forces that the child could perceive as a threat to his/her existence. The child's own feelings, which he/she is learning to express in the therapy environment, may threaten to overwhelm him/her. For example, the child might be frightened of not being able to control strong anger, strong sexual feelings, or strong dependency desires. If the child cannot manage these strong feelings and if the child has not developed full trust in the therapist's ability and willingness to prevent the child from being destroyed by these impulses, then he/she will freeze. The child also might become frightened of the therapist if the child becomes very dependent on the therapist before he/she develops trust that the therapist will not take advantage of his/her vulnerability.

In order to deal effectively with the child's resistance, the therapist needs first to appreciate the degree of threat the child must be experiencing to cause such frightened withdrawal (even if it is covered by a sullen anger) and then needs to convey to the child an acceptance of his/her anxiety. The therapist next attempts to understand the source of threat to the child. To achieve such an understanding is not always easy. The therapist draws on all sources of knowledge about the child—previous therapy session material, history, current family, school and peer problems—whatever might lead to a hypothesis about the source of the child's anxiety.

Once the source is determined, the therapist will not be able to reduce the child's anxiety much by simple reassurance (e.g., "Don't worry about growing into a baby again"); rather, the therapist arranges the environment, including him/herself, to protect the child from whatever is the perceived threat. For example, the therapist could bring the mother into the playroom to reassure the incompletely differentiated (from mother) child that the mother will not desert and therefore destroy the child. Or the therapist may hold a child who threatens to become over-whelmed by aggressive impulses, or *not* hold a child who is threatened with regressive pulls that might completely engulf and wipe out his/her individual existence.

In general, the message the therapist conveys to the child is "You are here and I am here, and I will help you learn that you can experience these frightening things without being annihilated."

How Does the Therapist Answer the Child's Questions about Other Children Who Use the Therapy Room?

Every time a child asks whether other children use the therapy room, he/she is asking about the relationship be-tween him/herself and the therapist. The child is attempt-ing to understand this new and strange relationship. It is not an easy relationship to understand. The unspoken questions about the relationship may be Is our relationship exclusive? Do I have to share you with other children? Do you have any children of your own? If you see many chil-dren, what makes our relationship so special? Are these my toys or do I have to share them (and you) with others? Do you like me as well as or better than those other chil-dren? Who in the world *are* you?

I try to answer the child's question directly and hon-estly. If the child asks, I tell the approximate number of children who use the room (not the names, of course) and the number of children seen by me personally. Asking the child why he/she asks the question will probably draw a blank, but the child's question might make a good entree to touch on the child's concerns about his/her relationship with the therapist. The therapist might push it a bit further with a comment such as "I guess it's sometimes hard to share the room or me." Or, "You would probably like to have the room and me all to yourself." You should not expect much, or any, response or discussion to follow such a remark, but it will let the child know you are in tune with some of his/her concerns. If the remark is untrue of the child's feelings at the moment, no harm is done; the child either ignores it or thinks, "Well, the guy[gal] is wrong, but he[she] is in there trying."

SHOULD YOU GIVE GIFTS AND SHOULD YOU RECEIVE GIFTS IN A PSYCHOTHERAPEUTIC RELATIONSHIP WITH A CHILD?

One position is that if you feel like giving a gift to your child client, do it. The argument is that if you like someone, it is natural to want to give that person a gift. Giving a gift is simply a way of showing affection for another person, so if you are fond of your child client, then why not be natural and give a gift to that child? There is one important difference between the therapy relationship and a real-life relationship: The therapy relationship is not mutual in meeting the psychological needs of each participant. The psychotherapeutic relationship is to satisfy the needs of the client, not the therapist. There are certain interpersonal behaviors that would be quite natural outside the therapy room but are not appropriate in a therapeutic relationship. The therapist must be extrasensitive to what the behavior means to the client. For example, if you feel like hugging someone of equal status in real life, you might just simply do it. If the person did not like it or attached too much meaning to it, that would be only 50 percent your responsibility, but if you hugged a client who did not like it or attached too much meaning to it, it would be 99 percent your responsibility. You, as a therapist, should know what the behavior means to the client and act according to the client's best interests, rather than to act according to what makes *you* feel good. So with exchanging gifts; the therapist should have a pretty good idea of what a gift exchange would mean to the child and then weigh carefully the answer to the question Is this in the best interest of the child?

The opposite position is to exchange *no* gifts. The argument for this position is that if you do not know what the gift means to the child, then you should play safe and not give it. The problem with this position is that not giving a gift and refusing to accept a gift are also behaviors that may not be in the best interests of the child. In fact, there may be cogent therapeutic reasons why you would want to give or receive a gift. Some reasons might be the following: The young, concrete-thinking child may need a tangible indication that you care about him/her, especially if the child is accustomed to this means of communication; refusing a gift may be totally baffling and hurtful to a child; if you are using a behavioral model, you might give small gifts as rewards for accomplishing some target behavior.

Over the years I have established some middle-of-the-road rules of thumb for myself that you might consider.

On Giving

1. Give a gift to a child client only if you want to convey a message to the child, such as "I care for you," and if it does not put the child under any obligation to return a gift to you. Be sure the gift is of small monetary value, so that if the child does feel an obligation to return a gift, it is not a burden.

2. If there are no dietary contraindications, a consumable gift such as a food treat has several advantages: (a) food treats are almost universally liked by children, (b) food is less likely to put the child under obligation because

he/she does not take home a visible product, and (c) a consumable gift symbolizes the temporary nature of the therapeutic relationship. If you give a more permanent gift, that may somehow convey a message that you expect the relationship to last forever.

3. If a small item strikes you as "just exactly right" for the child, do not obsess yourself into paralysis about the meaning of the gift to the child; trust your instincts a bit and do it.

Michael and I had been building models in the days when plastic models were first on the market. He taught me all I know about model building. Michael loved motorcycles, but at that time there were no motorcycle models on the market in Denver. On a trip to Philadelphia I spotted a plastic motorcycle model in a shop window and *had* to buy it for our work together. He was thrilled; we built it together, and he took it home. Presumably, he is not suffering today from the trauma of that event.

On Receiving

1. If parents ask you, suggest to them that they not bother to have the child give you a gift unless the child really pushes for it.

2. If the child insists and if you are given the opportunity for some input on gift selection (which is usually not the case), then urge something simple like a small box of candy, a handkerchief, or better yet, something the child has made.

3. When the child gives you a gift, accept it graciously and gratefully, since he/she would probably not understand and would be hurt by a refusal, particularly if the child made the present. If you can possibly display the gift over the next few weeks, the child will know that you really do appreciate and value the gift and the thought behind it.

What Can You Do if a Child Tells You He/She Is Going to Run Away?

The very fact that a child tells you he/she is going to run away is a demand for some kind of response from you. Does the child want you to stop him/her from running? Is the child expressing hostility toward you by forcing you into a stressful position? Is the child seeking attention and nurture from you? Is the child shouting out a message to his/her parents? Does the child want you to intervene in a parent–child struggle in which the child feels powerless?

First, you need to assess the level of danger to the child. Factors to consider are the child's age and maturity, the child's means of running away, the thoroughness and practically of the child's plans, and the safety of the place to which the child is planning to run. A runaway threat in therapy is one of the few instances where the child's safety takes precedence over the therapist-client confidentiality. If you believe the child is at risk of being harmed, then you must report it to the parents and, if you judge the child is in imminent danger, to the police. Even if your state child abuse law does not specify reporting a runaway, you are at risk of being liable if the child does run and is subsequently harmed. To preserve your relationship with the child, you need to let him/her know that you are reporting, to whom and why.

If the child tells you of the runaway plans early in the session, you might choose to dig for underlying causes before reporting. It would be fast therapy work, but it is just possible that you could defuse the situation in one session, at least enough to reduce significantly the likelihood of the child actually running. An understanding of the conflicts and feelings the child is having that led to this desperate step, whether it is done in one session or requires more, calls for hard work on both your and the child's part. Assuming the child is sending a message, what is the message and for whom is it meant? Usually the conflict underlying a desire to run away is an interpersonal conflict most often with the parent(s). When this is the case, a parent–child session or series of sessions is indicated, the goal of which would be to clarify the conflict and work out alternative solutions. Being the child's advocate, you can help empower the child to communicate his/her position and feelings to the parent and effect some change in the impasse.

Occasionally, an older child or adolescent will run away and then contact you by phone. If the child tells you where he/she is or comes to your office for a session, you need to be aware of your legal liability in case you do not report his/her whereabouts and the child is later harmed. In most states running away is no longer a status offense, but you want to be sure that the child is not in danger. In a spirit of openness, I would tell the child about my concerns and urge the child to contact his/her parents so I would not have to. If you have legal questions about any particular aspect of the runaway situation and your part in it, you could contact your local district attorney's office or Community Research Center, University of Illinois at Urbana-Champaign, 505 East Green Street, Suite 210, Champaign, Illinois 61820 (217) 333-0443.

WHAT DO YOU DO IF YOU LEARN ABOUT OR SUSPECT CHILD ABUSE?

Every state in the United States now has a law requiring report of child abuse, so the therapist really has no choice about reporting known or suspected child abuse. Physical and sexual abuse is one of the toughest issues a child psychotherapist can face, because reporting may terminate the helping relationship with the child and family. Because of wanting to continue in a position to help a family, I have often wished, in a short-sighted way, that we did not have child abuse reporting laws. Clearly, though, these laws represent a real advance in our society.

Most abusive behavior represents a cry for help by the parents. Although veiled, their mistreatment of their child(ren) is a desperate way of asking to be stopped from hurting their child(ren) further. Abusive parents are abused children grown up, and once one hears of their own impoverished personal histories, it becomes understandable how they came to be involved in abusive behavior. By and large, abusive parents do not want to treat their children badly.

There are some things you as the child therapist can do to cut down on the risk of doing more harm than good. Acquiring detailed knowledge of the child abuse law and crisis procedures in your state seems the sensible starting place. It is helpful to have a copy of the law, not only to become generally familiar with it but as a reference for particular points as they arise around a specific case. Recently, for example, I had to look up exactly how many years apart siblings had to be in order for their sexual behavior to be considered reportable sexual abuse. Especially useful would be to know how child abuse is defined in your state, on what kinds of information one bases a suspicion, who must report, what protection you have against a liability suit, and what the penalty is for not reporting. Another very important piece of information to have when helping kids and their families is a sense of what happens from the time of the first call reporting abuse until resolution. The best way I have found to obtain this knowledge is to call the number to which you report the abuse (family crisis center, child abuse hot line, whatever it may be called in your area) and set up a visit for yourself in that office. At that visit your contact worker can walk you through the procedure, indicating the various choice points and what may happen at each. If you know what the child and family will be experiencing, you have invaluable information for helping them cope with, at best, a difficult experience.

So how can you help the family? When you think there might be a possibility of child abuse in a new case, it would be prudent to state clearly to the parents and the child the reality of the reporting law. This can best be done at the first appointment when going over the mechanics of therapy, e.g., fees, conditions of confidentiality, and so on. If that prevents the family from continuing the connection with you or your clinic, so be it. When a family breaks off contact with you under these circumstances, it would be in the child's best interest to report what happened back to the referral source. If, however, the family continues working with you and if child abuse indeed does come up, they are less likely to feel betrayed when you report it.

When I think a child client might be abused or at risk of being abused, I generally proceed as follows:

1. When a child tells me he/she is abused, I believe it. Children rarely make up allegations of abuse. To finally risk telling an adult they are being abused and to not be believed puts the children under enormous pressure and further perpetuates abuse by "the system."

2. I will consult with a colleague about the case, especially if the evidence for abuse is indirect, because I may not want to believe that child abuse is really going on. There is almost always a strong wish that abuse is not occurring, because I do not want to see the child harmed and I want to avoid the inevitable stress to the family (and to myself) that follows a report of child abuse. When my colleague confirms what I do not want to hear, I'll take the next step.

3. The most critical message to convey to the child is that it is *not* his/her fault, that he/she is *not* being punished for being bad. The child needs to understand that there are problems in the family and that his/her mother or fa-

ther is having problems that are adult problems. I explain two important elements of the law to the child at whatever level the child can understand. These elements are that society says adults cannot harm children and that professionals must report abuse or be punished themselves. Also, I will explain to the child what is likely to happen: who will visit, the kind of questions they will ask, where they will take the child and for how long. To explain this, one needs to know about the different possibilities, given different levels of imminent danger to the child.

4. The same points next need to be made to the parents. I prefer to do this in person with the parents and to have the child present. If I do not tell a family everything I know about the circumstances in this case and what is likely to happen and then the parents find out something I did in secret, my chance to work with the family is gone. It is important to convey to the family that I have concern for them, that I want to continue working with them and their child, helping their family in any way possible.

5. I urge the parents to make the abuse report themselves, right there on the office phone. If the parents do not want to make the call, I'll ask them to stay while I do so. At the end of the call I'll ask the crisis worker what will happen next so I can inform the child and parents on the spot.

6. Assuming the parents are continuing to relate to me, I feel it is important to follow up the next day with a home visit or at least a phone call so the parents and the child will know that I am still concerned. This is clearly a time of crisis for the family, and extra sessions are not merely a gesture, but one hopes they can be used to support the child and the family.

These are meant to be suggestions; obviously, real cases do not go this smoothly and you may feel that the procedures I like to follow are all wrong for you and your situation. It is useful, though, to have some scenario in mind the first few times you are faced with a child abuse crisis so as not to be operating completely in the. dark in an emotionally charged situation.

Treating a child and a family in a child abuse situation is a complex affair and every child psychotherapist would be more competent if he/she obtained further knowledge and training in this area. The following are resources for obtaining information about the legal aspects of child abuse:

National Association of Council for Children
1205 Oneida Street
Denver, CO 80220
(303) 321-3963

National Legal Resource Center for
  Child Advocacy and Protection
American Bar Association
1800 M Street, N.W.
Washington, D.C. 20036
(202) 331-2250

Resources for obtaining information about the mental health aspects of child abuse:

Your nearest medical school; check to see if they have child abuse experts on their faculty.

The Henry Kempe National Center for
  Prevention and Treatment of Child Abuse
1205 Oneida Street
Denver, CO 80220
(303) 321-3963

Chapter 10

EVALUATION

HOW DO YOU EVALUATE TREATMENT PROGRESS?

Evaluating change in therapy has long been an extremely complex and difficult task. Typically, therapy outcome researchers have looked to three major sources for evaluation data: reports from the client (including psychological tests), reports of others who have frequent contact with the client (parent, teacher, therapist), and "objective" measures, such as measures of frequency of behavior, or external criteria, such as school or job achievement. Each of these sources has its limitations. The client may behave in a very different way but feel unchanged, or feel very differently but behave the same. His/her reports would most likely reflect changes in feeling. Observers may be biased due to some emotional involvement (parent) or vested interest (therapist). Objective measures may not reflect the client's improved or worsened subjective feelings. They might also be influenced by many factors outside of therapy, e.g., grades changing because of a change in teachers. Also, test results and behavior counts might not be too central to what is truly important in the client's life. Just as the careful researcher attempts to use several measures, so the therapist should obtain data from several sources in order not to be misled by one source of possibly skewed data.

The conscientious therapist systematically evaluates the client's progress, or lack of progress, in order to have some idea of the efficacy of the treatment method. The therapist has a contractual obligation to deliver a helpful service and an ethical obligation not to continue ineffective treatment.

The therapist trying to observe changes in therapy is a bit like the person concentrating on the minute hand of a watch in an attempt to detect movement. Similarly, changes in a child from session to session are usually impossible to see, but if anchor data are obtained at one point in time and the same order of data are obtained at longer-than-1-week intervals (minimum six weeks?), changes are more likely to be seen.

What kind of data should be obtained and from what sources? Obviously, this question has to be answered in terms of the original difficulties that brought the child into treatment. If the complaint was a specific symptom such as bed-wetting, not eating, truancy, or hitting the baby, the progress is relatively easy to measure if one can keep a running tally of the behaviors. In fact, since these behaviors occur outside the therapy room, there is no other way to measure progress than to go to the site of the behavior. If the behaviors could occur in the therapy room (cursing, temper tantrums, nervous habits, etc.) one would still need a record of behaviors outside of the therapy room, since the child may cease the behavior in the therapy room but not outside. For example, a child may not cling to the therapist any longer but continue to cling to the parent or the teacher. The external person with the greatest vested interest in changing the child's behavior (usually parent or teacher) may not be the most valid observer and recorder of behavior but is probably the most conscientious.

If the presenting complaint is more internal, relating to the child's feelings or attitudes, then progress is more difficult to evaluate. Feelings such as depression, anger, and fear may be displayed in the therapy room through behaviors associated with those feelings. The clinician is probably an imperfect counter of these behaviors but must do his/her best in using these behaviors to make judgments such as: Mark is less depressed than he was two months ago, Sally is just as nervous as when she started therapy, and Debbie is more angry than she was six weeks ago. If the therapist notes marked changes in mood, the child is probably demonstrating mood changes outside the therapy room but *one cannot automatically assume so.* Outside observers such as parents and teachers must be asked their judgments about any changes in the child's mood.

Attitudes such as self-denigration, dislike of teachers, or distrust of peers can often be obtained by direct questioning. As a supplement to the child's expressed attitudes, or particularly when the child cannot express his/her attitudes verbally, projective tests can be very useful. Interpretation of a single set of test protocols is often difficult, especially for the beginning student who does not have a large set of internal norms. Comparison of before-and-after test protocols is more reliable. One can simply count and compare, say, the number of negative statements about the teacher, scary stories, dependency themes, or themes of vulnerable, failing heroes.

Achievements by the child in the cognitive sphere are easier to evaluate. The following are three examples: (a) the child might learn that it is possible to both love and hate his/her father; (b) the child might understand that he/she is failing at school because of fear of what he/she thinks the teacher might say; and (c) the child might understand the reasons for his/her mother deserting the family. These cognitive changes are easy enough to evaluate; information or ideas that were not there are now present. What remains less clear is how well the child makes use of the new information or understanding. One would have to look for consequences of the cognitive changes. Consequences in the three examples above might be as follows: (a) the child reports less guilt about his/her anger toward father and is able to enjoy their time together more; (b) the child works harder at school and achieves more; and (c) the child feels less responsible for the mother's desertion because his/her perceived unloveworthiness was not the cause for the desertion.

The child may show changes for the better in areas other than those specified in the therapy goals. Possibly the therapeutic relationship was a factor in the observed changes, but the therapist must be careful not to take all the credit for normal growth and maturation. Even for changes toward the goals of therapy, the ascription of causes for those changes as lying within the therapy relationship is a highly tenuous exercise. One could say that all positive changes are due to the therapy and all negative changes the parents' fault, but presumably the statement would be made in jest. If positive changes occur in the direction of the therapy goals, the exact causal chain would be impossible to demonstrate in a single case. The therapist at this point must rely on theory to "explain" the observed events.

The evaluation of psychotherapy progress is often neglected and perpetuates the notion that this method of helping children is so much wishful thinking. We do not, in fact, have many well-designed and well-executed studies of the efficacy of child psychotherapy or any good research on the factors in the therapeutic process that effect change. This is all the more reason clinicians must keep careful records of treatment progress with each individual client.

One cannot fall back on the literature to say, "Well, if we just continue doing this, the child has an eighty percent chance of improving." The place to start this task is at the beginning of therapy when specific goals and methods of obtaining those goals are written. These goals and methods may be changed as the treatment progresses, but with such a list one at least has some kind of anchor point in a change continuum.

Chapter 11

TERMINATION

How Do You Know when to Terminate?

If the goal of therapy with the child is to change a behavior, removing unwanted behavior, or establishing desired behavior, then the therapy is completed when the target behavior is changed. If the goal, however, is to help the child by means of the therapeutic relationship to achieve greater independence and capacity to deal with stresses in life, then the answer to the question of when to terminate is more complex.

In Frederick Allen's excellent chapter, "The Ending Phase of Therapy" (Allen 1942; reprinted in Haworth 1964), he makes the point (p. 268) that when parents make the move to seek outside help for an impasse in their relationship with their child, this very move is the beginning of the end of the impasse. So if the goal of therapy is to help the child and parent achieve autonomy in solving their own problems, then the act of starting therapy is a large step in the direction of attaining such autonomy. Thus, the beginning of therapy is the beginning of the end of a problem. The therapist going into a therapeutic relationship with this attitude will be less likely to foster dependency than will the therapist who perceives him/herself as having the solutions to the client's problems.

Allen writes that the child will sense when he/she is ready to fly solo and will let the therapist know. The problem is that the child is seldom clear in his/her own mind when this time has come, let alone able to tell the therapist in so many words. Here are some clues the therapist might look for in the child as indications that the child has outgrown the therapeutic relationship and is getting ready to be more independent.

1. The child comes late or misses appointments. In cases where the child is brought to therapy by a parent, these late and missed appointments may be an expression of the parent's feelings about terminating therapy. In this case, the parent's therapist should bring up the issue of termination.

2. The child wants to leave the sessions early. This is noteworthy if the child has not done so before for some other reason.

3. The child brings a friend into therapy, if this has not been done before as resistance to dealing with painful issues that the child fears will come up.

4. The child discusses his/her relationship with the therapist, particularly if the child is not in the habit of discussing this relationship. Focus on the relationship indicates that the child is able to see the relationship with some degree of objectivity and is attempting to put it into perspective in terms of the rest of his/her life. Conceptualizing the existence of a relationship is a prerequisite for conceptualizing its cessation or nonexistence.

5. The child focuses more than usual on matters outside the therapy room, such as school, friends, family, past experiences, and plans for the future. Particularly note-

worthy are discussions by the child about what he/she would be doing were he/she not in the therapy sessions, e.g., playing with friends or watching a favorite TV program.

6. After many active hours with the material in the therapy room, the child begins to complain about there being nothing interesting to play with in the room.

7. The child begins recalling past times with the therapist in earlier therapy hours.

8. The child who has been using the play materials in a symbolic way begins to play out themes that suggest termination. Such themes could be of birth, independence, solving problems for self, leaving home, autonomy from adult figures who could represent the therapist or parent, constructing separate facilities for self and therapist, and being in control of interpersonal connections like bridges and the keys to doors.

9. The child expresses anger toward the therapist for no evident reason. The anger might be an expression of the child's understanding that at some level he/she is ready to terminate but becomes anxious or frightened about the idea and blames the therapist for throwing him/her out of therapy.

Some of these signs can be quite obscure. One problem in reading them is that the child seldom approaches termination with a single feeling. Most children ending therapy will have mixed feelings of fear, sadness, excitement about being more mature and independent, anger, and so on. Indeed, almost everyone has mixed feelings in ending any relationship. How the therapist and child deal with these feelings will be discussed in subsequent sections.

Although any one of these behaviors of the child may not signify a feeling of readiness to consider moving on and out of the therapeutic relationship, the therapist who is not emotionally overinvolved with the child—that is, who does not use the therapeutic relationship to meet his/her own emotional needs—will be alert to this possible meaning of any changes in the child's behavior. The therapist should from the onset of therapy always have the question in mind, "Is this an indication of the child's need to move on in life and away from our relationship?"

How Do You Deal with Premature Termination?

Often in real life the therapist and child do not have the opportunity to agree mutually on termination when the child is feeling strong enough to leave the relationship behind. The therapist might move to another town (especially early in the therapist's career with time-limited training assignments and new jobs), or the family might move out of town. For these kinds of reasons there is usually enough time before the separation date to have discussions with the child so he/she can understand the reason and to allow the child some expression of feeling about the separation and some time to work through (accept) some of these feelings.

If the family comes to the clinic knowing of some reason why sessions will terminate at a specific date, such as an impending move, limited financial resources, or short insurance coverage, then the therapist together with the family can decide whether this is enough time to really help the child. If time-limited sessions are started with everyone's knowledge of how many sessions are possible, then one could not expect the same depth of therapeutic relationship to develop between therapist and child. At times, however, such a limited number of sessions could speed up the process of the child's building independence precisely because he/she knows there is only a limited time to do so. I have seen rapid change associated with few sessions. Whether such change is the result of, or in spite of, the therapy is a question that single-case clinical research cannot answer.

One factor in deciding if short-term therapy should be undertaken is the nature of the presenting problem. If the problem is such that it would take a long time to resolve, then probably it would be best not to start, particularly if your short-term therapy would preclude the child's starting the needed longer therapy with someone else. Also, the child's problem might be of a nature that starting and stopping a relationship would be particularly harmful. It could be that a child who has experienced repeated rejections or a child who has basic trust problems might have feelings of unloveworthiness confirmed or belief in the untrustworthiness of others strengthened by a short-term relationship, particularly if the child cannot understand the external reasons for the termination.

More difficult to deal with, however, than planned early termination is the sudden, unexpected termination, such as that caused by serious illness of the child or therapist, the unexpected acquisition of a new job for the therapist or the parent, or the parents (for a variety of reasons) pulling the child out of therapy before the child is ready. In one unforgettable case of mine the mother of the 6-year-old boy discovered that he was becoming attached to me and very fond of coming to therapy. This gave her one more weapon in her bag of sadistic tricks to play on her child. With no notice, she withdrew the child from therapy. The experience is unforgettable for me because of my unresolved angry feelings and perhaps unforgettable for the boy because of his hurt feelings. I did meet the boy by accident on a school playground two years later, and it was a joyful reunion. It is difficult to assess the depth of the scars of such a ruptured relationship.

Unexpected terminations can cause pain for sure. The best the therapist can do is attempt to have at least one final session with the child or, if that is impossible, contact by phone or mail, in which the realistic reasons for termination are explained to the child and the positive good wishes from the therapist to child are conveyed. It would be appropriate in most cases, also, to leave the door open for future visits by the child.

The beginning therapist often asks whether it might be best *not* to form a close relationship with a child because of the hurt when the relationship ends. This is another form of the poet's question, "Is it better to have loved and lost than never to have loved at all?" The answer in life, as well as for child psychotherapy, comes from faith. For me, the answer lies in the belief that a child can grow and mature in a relationship with an adult who accepts the child unconditionally and that living through the pain of separation can be, in itself, a maturing achievement for the child. Of course there are times, especially in premature termination, when the pain outweighs the growth-fostering advantages. But life is not risk-free. To avoid all possible pain, one would not form relationships. One should stay alone in bed to be perfectly safe—except that is not so safe either, considering the number of people who die in bed.

HOW AND WHEN DO YOU TELL THE CHILD ABOUT TERMINATION?

Ideally, the child will let the therapist know in a direct or, more likely, in an indirect way when he/she is ready to stop therapy. If the child gives clues about termination, then you simply reflect to the child that he/she might be ready to stop therapy. More often, however, the therapist looks 2 to 3 months ahead to the summer vacation (the therapist's or the family's) or to another kind of holiday break and says something like, "How long do you believe you would like to continue coming in here for our sessions?" This question directs attention to termination but also lets the child know that he/she has a say in the matter. If the child answers, "Forever," you might say, "Forever, wow! That would be nice in a way, wouldn't it? Can you imagine when you are sixty and I am eighty-five years old we are still here playing? I guess you are really saying that you enjoy coming to our sessions and that you do not like to think about seeing them come to an end. Me too. I wish it didn't have to end." That might be enough for one session. At least you will know how the child feels about ending, depending on his/her behavior following this conversation. Perhaps, then, if there is time, you could let the topic lie for two to three sessions before bringing it up again for the child to contemplate. Each time be sure to read the child's answer and allow for mixed feelings in the child (see next section).

If the therapy has been time-limited from the onset, be sure the child knows at the first session how many sessions are planned. Then you might remind the child three or four sessions before and again two and one session before the last session. If the child had planned the termination date with you, then he/she simply needs a reminder as the agreed-on termination date draws near.

How Do You Deal with the Child's Feelings about Termination?

The child is likely to have a mixture of feelings about ending the therapy relationship. A common reaction, of course, is sadness at the loss of a valued relationship. The child could feel rejected, which might generate anger at the therapist or feelings of unloveworthiness. On the positive side, perhaps the child feels relief at ending a painful or boring relationship. The child might feel excitement about the future, about being "on my own." The freedom, the newly found autonomy, and the competence at handling stress better could produce feelings of pride. On a more concrete level, the child simply might be glad not to come to the therapy sessions so he/she does not have to travel through city traffic or so he/she can be doing something more interesting like playing with friends. In all likelihood the child will be having more than one of these emotional reactions to termination.

How you help the child deal with these feelings will depend on how you have been dealing with feelings all along in the therapy. You probably would not shift tactics just to deal with feelings around ending therapy. If the goal has been to help the child master situations, including managing his/her own feelings, then you would continue in that vein. First, the child would be allowed or encouraged to express the feelings, verbally or through play. Then the child would be helped to own the feelings. One way to help the child express and own feelings is to model the expression and owning of these feelings in yourself, especially if you can honestly identify some simultaneous negative and positive feelings so the child may see that it does not have to be all one or the other. Caution must be exercised that in doing so you do not burden the child with your feelings, so that he/she does not feel responsible for either causing them or for helping you deal with them. You are simply mentioning your feelings in order to give the child permission to have these or other feelings him/herself. But you probably would not start doing this unless you have been using this technique all along.

Since the negative feelings tend to overpower and crowd out the positive feelings, you might want to focus on the child's positive feelings, i.e., encourage the child to express and talk about positive feelings. This is not to deny the negative feelings that have been expressed, but to balance them with the more positive ones. One can thus try to end on an upswing, which probably would be more comfortable for both you and the child.

You are not limited to direct expression as the only way to help the child deal with feelings. Cognition may be used. In fact, the cognitive theorists tell us that restructuring the meaning of events in life, viewing events differently, changes emotions. Here are two ways in which the child may gain a different perspective on the relationship and thus on ending it: (a) you could discuss, with the child's help, changes that you and the child have seen in his/her life since therapy started, and (b) you could direct the child's attention to the future. Discuss potential future events and how the child will deal with them. These processes should help the child gain some distance and a new perspective on him/herself and the relationship.

To help the chid obtain some closure on the relationship, you might review some of your past experiences together. This is a natural occurrence when two adults end a regular relationship. Many children will do this spontaneously during the last session. Several times I have been astounded by children's memory as in the last session they go through in rapid succession and correct sequence all of the play themes of the past 5 to 8 months of therapy. When the children acted out the last eposide, it was the perfect place to say good-bye and leave, which they did.

One final and important point about helping the child deal with termination is, I believe, that the door should remain open for the child to return to see the therapist if he/she desires. Usually children do not, but if they know that they can, then the ending of therapy is not so painful, perhaps because it is not so final. This possibility of returning simply on request was not so clear to one of my recent clients. About 2 months after termination the boy's school principal telephoned to complain that he was suddenly acting terrible: fighting on the playground, sassing and cursing his teachers, and refusing to do his schoolwork. These were the very behaviors that brought him to therapy in the first place. On his return to the clinic I asked him why he was starting to do all those old things again. "I wanted to see you," he said. The behaviors faded off rapidly as he started regular therapy sessions again. He continued for 2 months before he was again ready to terminate but this time with a clear understanding that he could return to see me simply by calling for an appointment.

How Do You Deal with Your Own Feelings about Termination?

The mixture of feelings about termination the child might have, which are discussed above, are also feelings you are likely to have. If you do not have any of them, then you should ask yourself if this is the right profession for you.

The child therapist must walk a tightrope between overinvolvement and detachment, neither side of which makes a very good therapist. You, the child therapist, should be emotionally stable enough and have sufficient sources of psychological gratification outside the professional role that you do not need to obtain gratification primarily from clients. On the other hand, if you remain emotionally detached from your child clients, you will not be effective in helping them, no matter what model and which techniques you use. Research results indicate that adult clients' perceptions of their therapists' warmth, empathy, acceptance, autonomy-giving, and other personality characteristics account for a great deal of the variance in therapy outcome. Perhaps the same is true for child clients.

So if you are an effective therapist, you will become emotionally involved, and naturally you will have feelings in terminating with a child with whom you have grown close. The only suggestion I have is that as you have helped the child focus on the more positive feelings, so you might focus on those feelings in yourself: joy at seeing the child more mature and autonomous, pride at having played some part in the change the child has made, hope that the future will be good for the child, and trust that the child will feel able to return to see you if the need arises. The painful emotions of ending a relationship you will simply have to chalk up as part of living.

The feelings I am experiencing now at the termination of this work are hope that it may be of some use to you, the beginning therapist, and relief as I place the last dot.

SELECTED BIBLIOGRAPHY

Allen, F. H. 1940. *Psychotherapy with Children*. Reprint. Lincoln, NB: University of Nebraska Press.

Axline, Virginia. 1947. *Play Therapy*. Boston, MA: Houghton Mifflin.

Axline, V. M. 1964. *Dibs: in Search of Self*. Boston, MA: Houghton Mifflin.

Bixler, R. H. 1964. Limits are therapy. In *Child Psychotherapy*, edited by M. R. Haworth. New York: Basic Books.

Blackham, G. J., and A. Silberman. 1975. *Modification of Child and Adolescent Behavior*. 2d ed. Belmont, CA: Wadsworth Publishing Co.

Cooper, S., and L. Wanerman. 1977. *Children in Treatment: A Primer for Beginning Psychotherapists*. New York: Brunner/Mazel.

Dreikurs, R. 1964. *Children the Challenge*. New York: Hawthorn Books.

Erikson, E. H. 1959. *Psychological Issues: 1. Identity and the Life Cycle*. New York: International Universities Press.

Freud, A. 1946. *The Psychoanalytic Treatment of Children*. London: Imago.

Freud, A. 1977. *The Psychoanalytic Study of the child. Psychoanalytic Assessment: The Diagnostic Profile.* New Haven, CT: Yale University Press.

Ginott, H. G. 1964. The theory and practice of "therapeutic intervention" in child treatment. In *Child Psychotherapy,* edited by M. R. Haworth. New York: Basic Books.

Harter, S. 1977. A cognitive-developmental approach to children's expression of conflicting feelings and a technique to facilitate such expression in play therapy. *Journal of Consulting and Clinical Psychology* 45:417–432.

Harter, S. 1982. Cognitive-developmental considerations in the conduct of play therapy. In *Handbook of Play Therapy,* edited by Schaefer, C. E. and O'Conner, K. J. New York: Wiley.

Haworth, M. R., 1964. *Child Psychotherapy.* New York: Basic Books.

Jourard, S. M. 1971. *The Transparent Self.* 2d ed. New York: Van Nostrand Reinhold.

Kaplan, L. J. 1975. Testing nontestable children. *Bulletin of the Menninger Clinic* 39:420–435.

Kessler, J. W. 1966. *Psychopathology of Childhood,* chaps. 14–16. Englewood Cliffs, NJ: Prentice Hall.

Klein, M., 1949. *The Psychoanalysis of Children.* London: Hogarth Press.

McDermott, J. F., and S. Harrison. 1977. *Psychiatric Treatment of the Child.* New York: Jason Aronson.

Menninger Foundation, Children's Division. 1969. *Disturbed Children.* San Francisco: Jossey-Bass.

Moustakas, C. E. 1953. *Children in Play Therapy.* New York: Ballantine Books.

Moustakas, C. E. 1959. *Psychotherapy with Children: The Living Relationship.* New York: Harper & Bros.

Moustakas, C. E. 1972. *The Child's Discovery of Himself.* New York: Ballantine Books. (Former title: *Existential Child Therapy.*)

Murphy, L. B. 1962. *The Widening World of Childhood.* New York: Basic Books.

Santostefano, S. G. 1971. Beyond nosology: Diagnosis from the viewpoint of development. In *Perspectives in Child Psychopathology*, edited by H. W. Rie. New York: Aldine-Atherton.

Schaefer, C. 1976. *Therapeutic Use of Child's Play*. New York: Jason Aronson.

Schaefer, C., and H. Millman. 1977. *Therapies for Children*. San Francisco: Josey-Bass.

Swanson, F. 1970. *Psychotherapists and Children*. New York: Pittman.

Szurek, S. A., and I. N. Berlin. 1967. *Training in Therapeutic Work with Children*. Palo Alto, CA: Science and Behavior Books.

INDEX